Commercial Floristry

Designs and Techniques

SANDRA ADCOCK

Commercial Floristry
Designs and Techniques

SANDRA ADCOCK

THE CROWOOD PRESS

First published in 2012 by
The Crowood Press Ltd
Ramsbury, Marlborough
Wiltshire SN8 2HR

www.crowood.com

British Library Cataloguing-in-Publication Data
A catalogue record for this book is available from the British Library.

ISBN 978 1 84797 377 1

Acknowledgements

My thanks go to Oasis, provider of floral products,
who kindly sponsored much of the floral foam and sundries.

Also to Sue Paper ICSF for her guidance and advice, and for patiently proof reading the different floral designs and copy.

But my biggest thanks goes to my amazing, long-suffering husband Steve Adcock, who built a makeshift photography studio in the garage, and who took all the fantastic photographs, over 4,000 shots, which he then edited until we shortlisted them to the enclosed book. And not forgetting my daughter Tamsyn, who supplied endless cups of tea to keep me warm during the winter months outside!

Diagrams by Charlotte Kelly.

Dedication

I wish to dedicate this book to my father, who sadly passed away during its writing, and so was never able to see or read it.

Typeset by Sharon Dainton, Isis Design.
Printed and bound in Malaysia by Times Offset (m) Sdn Bhd.

Contents

Acknowledgements   4

Introduction   7

1   The Journey of a Cut Flower   9

2   The Preparation and Conditioning of Flowers   17

3   The Elements and Principles of Design   23

4   Tied Designs   35

5   Arrangement Designs   59

6   Wedding Designs   81

7   Function Designs   119

8   Funeral Designs   137

9   Seasonal Designs   175

Glossary   190

Index   191

Introduction

The industry of floristry is strenuous: long hours are frequently required due to the short life of the cut materials, the florist is often standing in a cold environment, and the levels of pay are low. But there is no other career that offers such daily variety and allows such creativity of designs: from a single flower purchase from a son to his mum, to a welcome bouquet to celebrate a new-born baby, to a funeral design saying goodbye to a loved one or a corporate design for a conference table. A florist deals with the highs and lows of family life and corporate events, helping to celebrate these milestones with appropriate floral designs.

In addition to this a florist has one of the most fantastic products on the high street: flowers change with the seasons, and as new cultivars are developed, so the variety available increases. It is also such a creative industry – though be warned, because once you are involved in this industry it will become part of you, and you will become a part of that community proudly calling themselves florists.

This book is aimed at supporting and helping students in their quest to learn and improve their skills in the art of commercial floristry. It is not intended as a substitute for college training, but should be used alongside formal tuition to help underpin knowledge gained at college establishments. The designs and information herein is aimed at beginner level and should support most beginner qualifications. It is essential in the current economic times that good product knowledge together with design skills are learnt and put into practice.

I consider myself very lucky that both my favourite occupations are combined in my daily routine: teaching about, and working with, flowers. This book sets out to explain the basic skills required to create commercial designs with step-by-step information supported by photographs and relevant information. Then once you have mastered the basic skills, let your creativity and product knowledge allow you to create fabulous designs.

LEFT: Rose buttonhole.

Chapter 1
The Journey of a Cut Flower

The cut flower often has a complex journey before it arrives safely in the hands of the florist. Flowers are grown and harvested across the world; the largest flower grower in the world is Holland. Other countries that specialize in particular flowers are Thailand and Malaysia, known for their orchids, Colombia for roses and carnations, and African countries for roses, to name but a few.

From the growers, the flowers are then transported over land or/and sea to their end destination. Many go via the large auctions in Holland. At auction the cut flowers are purchased by wholesalers and distributed to their wholesaler outlets across the world. In the next chapter we will further explore the use of flower food to enhance the transportation process, and the essential method of preparing flowers and foliages ready for commercial use called 'conditioning'.

At auction, flower prices fluctuate according to demand on the day, and this can lead to dramatic price rises on some individual products. It is essential therefore that a florist becomes aware of 'peak periods', where demand for particular products is high and where correspondingly the price reflects this.

Another factor that affects the price of flowers is their seasonal availability: although in this 'high tech' scientific age it is possible to obtain flowers out of their natural growing season, you will pay a hefty premium for this. Knowledge of the seasonal availability of flowers will therefore save you and your customer money, and you will be able to obtain strong stems and good-sized blooms due to the fact that the flower is within its natural growing season.

An important factor to bear in mind in this age of environmental awareness is a flower's carbon footprint, and a florist can research locally grown products or fair trade products that benefit either the environment or local communities. There are still English-grown flowers available, the most notable being freesia, iris,

PEAK PERIODS

In the UK there are several peak periods:

Valentine's Day, 14 February: There is a high demand for all red flowers but especially red roses, and roses in general will be more expensive.

Mother's Day, the third Sunday before Easter: Most flowers and plants have a premium price leading up to and over the weekend concerned, particularly in pastel colours, and roses and lilies remain universally popular.

The Jewish New Year (Rosh Hashana), in late September/ early October (if your shop services a Jewish community): Planted baskets and containers with long-lasting designs are very popular, as well as flowers.

Christmas: There are no deliveries on Christmas Day, but the month of December increases in activity and demand until Christmas Eve, with red and white flowers and gold and silver designs often requested together, and with a much increased use of ivy, holly and mistletoe. Plants such as cyclamen, poinsettia and azalea, and also advent designs, are popular at this time of year. However, be aware that the auction houses close over this period, so fresh flowers can be difficult to obtain between Christmas and the New Year.

The wedding season: Traditionally this runs from early June to late September, although with more venues besides houses of worship gaining their wedding licences this trend could change. White and cream roses and lilies, including calla lilies and hydrangeas, can become more expensive. Wholesalers should be able to advise on predicted prices, especially if a particular flower is required.

In addition to the UK peak and high demand periods, due to the global nature of auctions, be aware that prices fluctuate over European peak periods that are often not the same as the UK dates, but impact on the prices paid by UK wholesalers.

LEFT: A Valentine's Day bouquet.

chrysanthemums, alstroemeria and roses.

This book will also cover the responsible disposal of waste, and where possible recycling.

....

Plant and Flower Nomenclature

Plants and flowers can be referred to by both common and Latin names. The common name is the name by which a plant is commonly known, and often describes the appearance of the flower – for example snapdragon, or red hot poker. However, this can have two distinct disadvantages: firstly, common names can differ from one country to another, and there can even be national and/or regional variations; and secondly, the name does not specifically identify a particular colour. The botanical name overcomes this problem because it is recognized worldwide. It is broken down into two parts, genus and species, which are always in Latin, and may be further divided by cultivar (the name of any cultivated variety). For example:

Common name: lilac
Genus: Syringa
Species: vulgaris
Cultivar: 'Dark Koster'

Common name: stock
Genus: Matthiola
Species: incana
Cultivar: 'Carmen'

....

Buying Stock: Where and How

There are several ways that a florist can purchase their stock at wholesale prices, although be aware that wholesale outlets have minimum orders.

Via the Internet

A florist can set up an account with an internet florist wholesaler, or buy direct from the grower. Ordered stock can be delivered in a variety of ways, via postal courier or by lorry; sometimes by prior arrangement a shop can provide a key to the supplier who will deliver the order at any time of the day, and even during the night, so that the delivery is in the shop ready for the owner's attention.

Through Wholesalers

A florist can apply initially for a business account with a wholesaler, and once this has been set up, can pre-order flowers (for weddings in particular) and collect them or have them delivered. In addition during opening hours the florist can visit the wholesaler and select what he wants from amongst a vast range of fresh products from the current delivery, and anything else he might need besides, such as vases, tools, foam frames, and drive them back to his shop.

Flying Dutchman/Visiting Salesperson

'Flying Dutchman' is the term applied to the large refrigerated lorries, owned by independent wholesalers, which drive directly to shops by prior arrangement on a daily/weekly/monthly basis. These

WHOLESALE AND RETAIL PRICES

The 'wholesale price' is the term used to describe the price that shops pay for their cut flowers/ foliages and other products. Prices are quoted excluding VAT.

The 'retail price' is the term used to describe the amount the shop charges the customer once they have added their percentage and VAT.

provide an essential link for those florists who are not near a wholesaler.

Students wishing to purchase their own flowers would not be able just to pop into their local wholesaler, as these are exclusively for business owners. Students are advised to seek guidance from their college as to who could inform them about any special arrangements – for example they might be able to buy from the college itself, or take advantage of special agreements with their own wholesalers.

Ordering Flowers and Foliages

When ordering from their provider florists must be aware that there are certain commercial amounts in which specific flowers are generally ordered. Flowers are freighted in different ways – some are transported packed flat in boxes, some upright in water, and some in individual phials of water – but most are bundled into bunches or wraps of five, ten, twenty, twenty-five or fifty, depending on the variety, and in the main all contained in a cellophane sleeve. This is how they are sold; they can also be sold by weight (the table opposite is only a guide, since amounts could differ from one wholesaler to another).

....

Tools of the Trade

Professional floristry requires a set of relevant tools and equipment; these can be sourced through the college provider or a specialist wholesaler who supplies the trade (you may need to have a minimum spend). Your equipment can be stored in a small portable toolbox, which can be purchased from your local hardware shop. A few of these tools are essential to help condition fresh stock and to create professional designs. Much of the equipment is inexpensive, and you can build up your toolkit gradually over time.

Fresh materials	Amounts
Alstroemeria	Tens
Anthurium	Various amounts depending on your wholesaler. Small bouquets of three Box of twelve – medium heads Box of sixteen – large heads
Antirrhinum	Tens
Arachniodes adiantiformis	Twenties
Bouvardia	Twenties
Brassica	Fives
Chrysanthemum – bloom	Tens
Chrysanthemum – spray	Fives
Cymbidium orchid	Single stems
Dendrobium	Tens
Dianthus	Twenty-fives
Dianthus spray	Fives
Delphinium	Tens
Eucalyptus	By weight
Eustoma	Tens
Freesia	Fifties
Galax leaves	Bags of 250
Gerbera – large	Various amounts depending on your wholesaler Racquets of ten Box of fifty
Gladioli	Tens
Gypsophila	Twenty-fives
Iris	Fifties
Lillium	Tens
Limonium – misty	Twenty-fives
Rosas	Twenty-fives
Ruscus	Fifties
Tulipa	Fifties
Zantedeschia	Tens, and fives for larger ones

Cutting Tools

Floristry scissors: There is a whole range of specialist scissors, essential for cutting and conditioning soft and semi-woody stems and low gauge wires. Keep a separate pair of scissors for cutting ribbons, cellophanes and organza.

Floristry knives: Again, a range of knives is available; a regular florist's knife can be used to cut foam into shape, or to condition flowers and foliages by cutting the stems diagonally to encourage maximum intake of water. A long-bladed knife is very useful for cutting large blocks of wet foam into desired shapes.

Secateurs: Essential for cutting through tough woody stems; it has comfort grips and a security lock when not in use.

Wire cutters: For cutting heavier gauge wires and artificial flower stems.

Pliers: Useful for wirework where a strong and secure twist of wire is needed.

Thorn strippers: A useful tool to help quickly remove thorns from stems.

Foliage strippers: Another useful aid to defoliating stems.

Floristry cutting tools.

Floristry fixing mechanics.

Tying aids.

Fixing Tools/ Equipment

Pot tape: Available in two colours, green and white, and two widths, 6mm and 12mm. These tapes are used for fixing foam to containers; the wider one is used where more strength is required.

Floristry stem tape: There are two different types of tape, with the same purpose of concealing wires, sealing in stem ends and covering sharp wires: first a stretchy self-sealing tape with the registered brand name of Parafilm, and the other a sticky crêpe-like tape used in the main under the registered brand name Stemtex.

Stem tape: This tape is available in two green tones, white and brown, although you may be able to obtain other colours from specialist cake makers (it is used for constructing sugar flowers).

Double-sided tape: This tape is useful for gift wrap or for securing leaf manipulation (sticky dots can also be used for this purpose).

Frogs: Used together with floral fix (a sticky green substance) to help fix and secure foam into containers.

Stapler and staples: For packaging and preparing funeral ribbon edging.

Hot glue gun and glue sticks: A versatile tool for sticking heavyweight materials together.

Floristry glue: A specialist cold glue that can be used for sticking fresh materials together, mainly for wedding work.

Tying Aids

Green twine: String used for tying stems in hand-tied designs, or for the basis of lightweight garlanding.

Reel wires.

Paper-covered wire: Again, useful for securing hand-tied designs or binding stems together where more strength is required.

Polypropylene twine: A lightweight twine used for tying stems.

Floristry Wires

Stub wires: These come in different gauges depending on their intended use (see Wiring techniques) – 0.32mm, 0.56mm, 0.71mm and 0.90mm. For very heavyweight purposes 1.20mm may be required.

Reel wires: These come in 0.32mm gauge for binding and support techniques, and 0.56mm for binding and support wiring where a heavier support is required.

Decorative wires: Available in a host of different colours and weights to enhance modern work with ornate finishes.

Containers

A large range of plastic containers is available, suitable for securing wet or dry foam, depending on the required design. There are trays for one or two or more

Decorative wires.

Assorted floristry dishes.

blocks of foam, and circular trays for cut-down foam or foam cylinders. The trays can be purchased in green, black and white, and on occasion clear plastic. Specialist containers for candelabra can also be purchased, such as candle cups and candle holders and hanging design shovels.

Other Miscellaneous Equipment

Water mister/sprayer: An essential tool for spraying a fine mist of water onto fresh materials (as appropriate) to help keep them fresh.

Sachets of flower food: For the customer to add to the water of cut materials.

Floristry cards: Specialist cards covering a wide range of occasions, including funerals, birthdays, anniversaries, or expressing thanks or greetings. They come with envelopes for gift use or clear envelopes for funerals.

Floristry care cards: Specialist pre-printed cards providing the customer with instructions as to how to care for their floral design, whether it be cut flowers, tied flowers or a design in foam.

Floristry card pick: Used to attach the card to the design.

Bridal Accessories

Corsage badges: For gluing fresh or artificial materials.

Hair combs, Alice bands: For fixing either wired or glued materials directly onto flowers.

Floristry magnets: To attach corsages (be aware that they can interfere with pacemakers).

Floristry cards and flower food sachets.

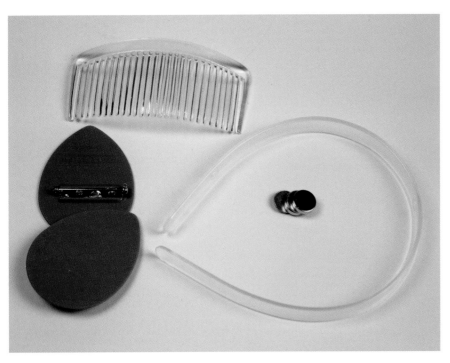

Floristry bridal accessories.

Health and Safety

Although floristry is not a high risk career, be aware of the potential risks that you and the public could be exposed to.

Clothing: Always wear appropriate clothing and footwear: footwear should be closed in style, thereby preventing damage to the feet should scissors or other sharp objects be dropped, or in the presence of thorns. Warm clothing is essential, especially during the winter months: most floristry shops adopt a low heat policy, with a low ambient temperature that is ideal for flowers – but not for people. Warm clothing is also vital for prolonged visits to the refrigerated sections of the wholesalers.

Tools: Keep all tools clean and sharp – bacteria build up on the blades of frequently used tools, which is harmful to both the flower and the florist. You are more likely to cut yourself on a blunt tool than a sharp one. Ensure that you know how to use all tools correctly.

Tetanus: Check that you are covered by a current tetanus jab. (Tetanus is an infection that can invade through open wounds or cuts.)

Correct lifting: Adopt good lifting procedures to protect your back from damage.

Toxic materials: Be aware of the potential toxic properties that certain flowers and foliages contain, and be sure to advise customers how to handle such materials (for example extra precaution is required with berried material near children and some pets). Always wash your hands before eating or drinking after you have handled cut materials.

Risk assessment: In a commercial or teaching environment an employer or teacher will be responsible for a risk assessment to ensure that all risks in the workplace are minimized, to ensure a safe working environment.

Insurances

Employers' Liability Insurance: This is a compulsory insurance if employing anybody, and it is advisable to use an approved insurance provider. This policy insures against liability for bodily injury or disease sustained by employees during the course of their employment.

Public Liability Insurance: Again, be sure to use an approved insurance provider. Public liability insures against the injury or accidental death of any person other than an employee while at work. It also provides cover against any damage incurred to the property of others.

Seek professional advice regarding the amount of insurance cover required – this will depend upon the size and nature of the business.

As a student be aware that any designs that you sell or install could be subject to litigation: if/when you get to this stage in your commercial career, ensure that you are appropriately insured.

Chapter 2
The Preparation and Conditioning of Flowers

2

Preparation before a delivery or collection of flowers is essential. A clean working space is required, and vases and buckets in a variety of sizes should be thoroughly washed and filled ready for use with suitable flower food. Appropriate tools which should be clean and ready to use include secateurs, scissors, knives, cloths and dustpan and brush. In addition protective clothing should be used – for example, gloves, so as to avoid prolonged exposure to plant sap, which can be an irritant to the skin. Tools should be clean and ready to use.

Conditioning Flowers

Conditioning is the procedure by which the florist prepares the cut materials ready to sell and ensures that they are in optimum condition – hence the term. There are different conditioning methods, but the order in which tasks are prioritized when conditioning flowers is often dependent on the type of stem structure you are dealing with. The conditioning process is essential to ensure maximum longevity of the flowers, and also to increase their presentation value – but carrying out the task without any thought to cleanliness and the correct storage methods will result in the early demise of the flowers and disappointment to both customer and florist.

Problems that can occur due to poor or ineffective conditioning and storage result from undue exposure to ethylene gas, and the deleterious growth of bacteria.

Controlling Exposure to Ethylene Gas

Ethylene gas is colourless and odourless, and is produced as plants decompose and fruit ripens; it is also a by-product of man-made processes such as combustion. It is harmless to humans, but if flowers are exposed to the gas it can dramatically shorten their lifespan, resulting in yellowing of the leaves, and flower and petal drop, and completely stopping any further development of the flower. Damage caused by ethylene gas is irreversible. Some flowers are incredibly sensitive to ethylene gas exposure, such as dianthus (carnations), antirrhinums, alstroemeria and orchids.

The presence of ethylene gas, and therefore the exposure of flowers to it, can be minimized by following these few guidelines:

- Keep flowers away from obvious sources of the gas, such as car pollution, fruit and decaying plant material.
- Maintain good ventilation in the storage area, ensuring a good flow of air around materials so as to prevent any build-up of gas.
- Store flowers at a low temperature – ethylene gas occurs more at warmer temperatures.
- Remove dead flowers and old leaves from stock.

Controlling the Growth of Bacteria (Botrytis)

Bacteria can be readily introduced to cut stems via dirty tools and water. It is essential to minimize the risk of the growth of bacteria by observing the following tenets of good practice:

- Add the appropriate flower food to the water (see the notes on flower food in the later section Industrial Flower Storage), and refresh the water on a regular basis.
- Store in refrigerated units.
- Maintain good ventilation.
- Avoid cramming too many stems into the same bucket – the flowers' close proximity to each other will cause a rise in heat due to a process called transpiration, and decomposition will occur in this situation.
- Avoid getting flower heads wet, and if this occurs, give them a gentle shake to remove as much water as possible, then place them in a cold room or into cold storage.
- Remove any decaying material.
- Keep the whole storage environment clean.

Controlling the Environmental Conditions

When handling cut flowers the florist also needs to be aware of the environmental conditions to which the flowers will be exposed, and must pay particular attention to the effects of humidity, draughts, overcrowding, light and temperature.

HUMIDITY
Excessive humidity will lead to the growth of botrytis and the production of ethylene gas, which will cause the flowers to rot. It

is important to remove the cellophane packaging, as this will reduce humidity. In the hot summer months most plant material will benefit from being mist watered, though be careful not to overdo it.

DRAUGHTS
Excessive draughts will cause plant material to develop 'burn' marks, a brown discoloration of the leaves and flowers at their tips.

OVERCROWDING
Allowing adequate space around the stems of flowers and plants will improve and prolong their health. Overcrowding in buckets leads to temperature levels increasing, and therefore a greater likelihood of the spread of bacteria and the production of ethylene gas. If too many stems are forced into a bucket or vase, damage will occur when you try and remove a stem from the container.

LIGHT
Light will encourage some flower material to continue to grow, buds to open and flower heads to mature more quickly. This is useful to know if you wish to accelerate the opening process of flower heads so they can be used for certain designs, such as wedding or funeral work where open flowers are needed. Equally you can slow down the opening process by removing flowers from the light. Be aware that some flowers have a phototropic propensity, meaning that their heads and stems will grow towards the light – tulips are very prone to this phenomenon.

TEMPERATURE
The temperature needs to be governed carefully – too high, and the flower material will wilt and rot as a result of botrytis and exposure to ethylene gas; too cold, and petals and foliages will be vulnerable to frost burn.

The optimum temperature for most flower and foliage storage is 6°C.

Industrial Flower Storage

Specialist cold-room products, fridges and display units are available to store flowers at the optimum temperature. This type of refrigeration is different to a fridge designed for food in that the fans are controlled by a thermostat, which ensures that both a cooler and a more constant temperature is achieved. This prolongs the flowers' shelf life, and although the initial outlay is expensive, its main benefit is that the florist can work in advance of an event, since designs can be constructed and stored before their delivery date, and this in turn means that more orders can be taken and successfully fulfilled. There is also the further advantage that you can buy in bulk, which is generally cheaper anyway and involves fewer buying trips, thus saving both time and travelling costs.

Treating with Flower Food

After harvesting, cut flowers are treated with a variety of specialist flower foods; these have different roles to play over the harvesting, transporting and selling periods.

The wholesaler administrates the first of these specialist food treatments: this helps rehydrate dry-packed flowers, and no food nutrient is included; these flowers are normally then stored in a cold-room environment.

The next treatment of flower food is administered by the wholesaler: this one contains a limited amount of food, just enough to keep the cut stems at maintenance level, without overfeeding the blooms and causing them to 'blow', so they will last throughout the selling period.

The next specialist food is administered by the retailer/florist: this contains a high amount of food nutrient as well as a bacteria and ethylene gas inhibitor and a pH balancer, all to ensure maximum bud opening and flower development.

Lastly there is the consumer flower food, which helps to keep the health of the flower at a premium and encourages maximum level of flowering.

In addition the florist should be aware of other specialist flower foods on the market; these include:

* Bulb flower food – a specialist food for any cut bulb material such as hyacinthus, narcissus, convallaria (lily of the valley).
* Gerbera – a tablet food form used by the florist to help prevent, amongst other things, the bacteria/botrytis to which this flower is vulnerable.
* Bovardia – this flower comes with its own personal sachet, which should be used to ensure good hydration.

When using any of the above it is vital to read the manufacturer's instructions and to administer the correct dosage for maximum beneficial effect. Commercially there are dispensers that measure out the exact dosage required.

There are, of course, many other household remedies that claim to have amazing effects on flowers, such as coins, sugar, bleach and so on. However, these have not been scientifically researched and cannot be accurately measured in a vase or bucket.

General Conditioning Procedure

On receiving a delivery of flowers, check their condition: examine them for damage, broken heads, broken stems, temperature damage and pests, and if there are any problems report these to your wholesaler immediately. Also check them for any signs of distress – wilting heads and floppy foliage – and this will help you prioritize the order in which to start the conditioning process (see box panel).

Flowers should be conditioned in order of need or demand, according to the following priorities:

1. Distressed flowers – any plant material that shows signs of wilting or flaccidity.

2. Flowers required for urgent orders.

3. Long-stemmed flowers, as the water takes longer to travel up to the flower head.

4. Delicate flowers, such as freesia, eustoma.

5. Expensive flowers.

6. Dry-packed flowers with semi-woody stems, such as chrysanthemums.

7. Dry-packed flowers with woody stems, such as hypericum.

8. Flowers in their own water phials, such as orchids, anthuriums.

9. Foliages.

Most dry-packed flowers will need at least a couple of hours conditioning before they are ready for sale.

General Conditioning

Having unpacked your flowers, the general conditioning procedure is as follows, and is suitable for most items bought.

1. Remove any packaging, such as cellophane sleeves, with the exception of leather leaf plants, palms and anthuriums, as these require the humidity that the sleeves provide.
2. Check for damage – if botrytis or excessive broken heads are found, report this to your wholesaler.
3. Remove the lower leaves and thorns, taking care not to damage the outer epidermis of the stem – as a guide this means any material that would go under the water line. This prevents the leaves rotting underwater causing bacteria to build up in the water.
4. Re-cut the stems about 3.5cm from their end at a 45-degree angle, thereby increasing the surface area and allowing more water to be absorbed.
5. Immediately put the conditioned stems into lukewarm/room temperature water – flowers absorb warm water better, and it contains less oxygen (which can cause airlocks within the stem), having first ensured that the appropriate flower food has been added.
6. Place in a refrigerated/cool area (though be aware that not all flowers like such a cold environment – these will be covered later).

There are five different types of stem: woody, semi-woody, soft, latex and hollow. Examples of each type are as follows, and the general conditioning methods as described above should be observed unless indicated otherwise:
Woody stems: Forsythia, roses, most foliages.
Semi-woody stems: Roses, carnations.
Soft stems: Zantedeschia, orchids.
Latex stems: Euphorbia, ficus.
Follow points 1–4 of the general conditioning procedure described.

However, you will find that after cutting each stem, the latex sap will not stop leaching out and it will be necessary to seal the cut stem ends either by passing them through a flame for a few seconds (this cauterizes/seals the latex without preventing the uptake of water), or by placing just their tips into boiling water for a few seconds (being careful to protect the foliage and flower heads from the steam) – again this will cause the stems to seal. Then remove them and place them in fresh, tepid water (having added an appropriate flower food). Remember that this type of sap can be extremely irritant to the skin, so wear gloves.
Hollow stems: Delphinium, amaryllis.
Air locks can be a problem for this type of stem, with air becoming trapped inside the flower at the top of the stem. To prevent this happening, follow general conditioning points 1–4 (note that in point 4 you may need to use a knife to trim the stem, as scissors can crush the hollow stems and cause them to cave in), then turn the flower upside down and fill it with water that has been prepared with the addition of some flower food; then plug the base of the stem with cotton wool to stop the water draining back out. In certain instances it is possible to further support the hollow stem by inserting a stick inside it – this is especially helpful to the amaryllis due to the heavy weight of the open flower head.

Exceptions to the Rule

There are, however, some exceptions to the rule as regards conditioning procedure – here are a few of the most common, and how to accommodate their needs:
Tropical flowers: Curcuma, strelitzia, heliconia, anthurium, orchids.
Remove any individual plastic phials (wash and save these for future use – see later how to re-use them), re-cut the stems at a 45-degree angle, and store at room temperature: these flowers do not tolerate

cold temperatures or draughts, either of which would cause them to 'burn' and discolour, and would greatly reduce their longevity.

Gerbera: Use specialist gerbera flower food. These flowers are transported flat-packed and dry, and due to their soft stems need great care in handling when being rehydrated – it is essential that once the stem end is cut, the flower head and stem are kept upright: failure to do this will result in the rehydrated flower heads being held at very jaunty angles, making them difficult to use. The specially designed cardboard packaging and/or buckets with extensions that are provided to support the gerbera flower and stem will enable them to be conditioned correctly. Be aware that this hairy stem is vulnerable to botrytis, so keep the water clean and shallow in depth, and refresh it frequently.

Syringa (lilac): Buds must be showing colour. Remove any foliage – although this shrub is usually supplied without foliage – and provide it with its own specialized flower food; re-cut the stems, and repeat this process again later to help this woody stem rehydrate. This is a thirsty flower, so it is important to top up its water supply regularly.

Narcissus: This flower when conditioned releases a poisonous sap, which is very irritant; the sap is also poisonous to other flowers, so the narcissus must be conditioned separately. Allow it to stand for a while before use. Be aware that these flowers are sold dry in the wholesalers, and also frequently as such by florists, but as soon as they are put in water the flower heads will open; they can be left three to five days without water.

Hyacinth: Try to retain as much white bulb material at the base of the stem as possible, because this continues to rehydrate the flower.

Bouvardia: Follow the general conditioning method, but add the special sachet of food as supplied by the wholesaler. Cut the stems again if

necessary. Do not store at a temperature lower than 2–10°C, because this could cause the flowers to wilt.

Dianthus (carnation): When cutting the stems be careful not to cut through any of the nodes (the swollen joints in the stem)

because doing this will prevent the uptake of water – cut above or below them to ensure that water can be absorbed effectively.

Helianthus (sunflower): This is a thirsty flower, so be sure to top up its water

Gloriosa 'air bag'.

Removing 'paddles' from molucella.

supply regularly.

Gloriosa: This pretty flower arrives in its own individual 'air bag', which should be removed. Re-cut the stems and place the flowers in water with an appropriate flower food. Do not store them at a temperature below 6°C, as discoloration will take place. Limp flowers can be revived by submerging them in lukewarm water for a few minutes.

Zantedeschia (calla lily): Store this flower in a dark vase, because if the cut stem is exposed to daylight the end will curl up on itself.

Paeonia: Buy flowers with loose buds, but if any bud fails to open, hold it under a tap to remove the sticky layer that naturally accumulates. Always check that it has enough water, and refresh the water a couple of times a week.

Molucella: Follow the general conditioning procedure, but remove the top 'paddles' as these have a phototropic property. Re-cut the stems.

Revival Methods

Sometimes conditioning methods do not work and the flower still looks distressed (wilted) this is normally due to an air lock being contained within the stem. Drastic measures are then required.

Roses (prone to air locks) and woody stemmed materials – place cut stems into boiling water (protect heads and foliages from steam with card or paper wrapped round – this will also support any drooping heads) about 2.5cm (1in deep). Keep the stems in the water until the stem has rehydrated then cut off the 'boiled stem end', then put in bucket with tepid water containing flower food. Soft stems, such as Tulips – wrap tightly in paper, then re-cut stems and put packaged stems into prepared tepid water this supports the stems while they re-hydrate.

Immersion: some cut materials can absorb water through the cells that surround the stems and leaves so they can benefit from being fully immersed – however be aware that you must never immerse products that are grey or hairy leaves or waxy and fleshy flowers – this will discolour and stain them introducing them to bacteria.

Misting: again can be used to quicken the conditioning procedure by introducing water to the cells throughout the flower and foliage – but again do not mist grey or hairy leaves and certain flower heads – such as dark purple Eustoma – because the water will create marks and discoloration.

Stock rotation

It is important to observe good stock rotation practice, where old or short-lived stock is used first. Poor practice will result in a damaged shop reputation and loss of profit.

Mature stock should be kept aside for use in 'now' arrangements that require flowers to be at their fullest and best potential – eg. open lilies for funeral work and fully formed roses for weddings. Fresh flowers in bud would not be suitable for funeral work as the flowers would not be open on the day of funeral – but would be the right choice for a gift bouquet as the flowers will last a week or more depending on the flower choice.

A florist should aim to have satisfied customers. This is only achieved if the products they have bought are long lasting and look appealing. This is easily achievable if the conditioning, storage and stock rotation procedures are adhered to.

Stock Handling

In addition to knowing about conditioning procedures a florist should be well versed as to handling techniques to preserve the good health of their stock. First of all, always take care when removing individual items from buckets and vases,

carefully holding an individual flower under the flower head between finger and thumb, and giving the stem a little shake to release it. Some flowers get in a natural tangle however careful you are with them, gypsophila and freesia being prime examples of this – in this case you may need to remove all the stems from the buckets and lay them out on a table, then gently tease out the stems you require. Be especially careful with light-coloured flowers: any contact with the flower head should be avoided, as any bruising of the petals will cause them to discolour later.

Chapter 3
The Elements and Principles of Design

3

Flowers placed in either a container or vase without thought will always be just a random collection of flowers; however, when the 'elements' and 'principles' as explained in this chapter are applied, the way the flowers are selected becomes meaningful, a comprehensive design. There are five 'elements' of design, and these are the building blocks to a successful floral design. They may be identified as texture, colour, form, space and line; an easy mnemonic by which to remember them is: The Chelsea Flower Show London.

Texture

The unique characteristics and textural variety of plant materials adds a visual dimension to any design. All objects process texture, which can be further divided into two types: visual texture and actual texture. Actual texture is a texture that you can physically feel, whereas the florist is mainly concerned with the visual texture. Although in this case we may not touch a certain texture, our minds provide a sensory reaction – thus visual texture generates tactile sensation.

Good contrasts of texture ensure maximum appreciation, such as rough next to smooth. Some textures have greater dominance than others, such as a shiny texture, in which case use smaller amounts of the shiny texture with larger amounts of dull texture to create a visual balance. Texture is especially important when using all one colour in the same design, because this will increase the design's impact. This

EXAMPLES OF TEXTURE

In flowers, Nature provides us with a large range of textures:

Gypsophila, trachelium, dianthus	fluffy
Celosia cristata	crinkled
Eryngium	spiky
Anthurium	glossy
Strelitzia	waxy
Aspidistra	shiny
Liatris, nigella	hairy
Lilium, brassica	matt
Rosa	velvety
Asparagus	feather soft
Ananas	spiny
Sedum, echinops	dotty
Brunia	rough
Craspedia	dimpled

Design showing a variety of textures.

element can also apply to the texture of the container and any accessories used – for example a rough-textured container will increase the impact of an all-rose design because of the matt texture of the rose petals.

Be aware that to reveal plant texture to its best advantage good lighting is essential – poor lighting will not enable the viewer to distinguish between them.

Colour

Colour is often the most considered element of design, in that when a customer selects a floral display or bouquet it is usually its colour that dominates their decision. It is therefore vital that a florist fully understands colour and how to use it to best effect.

Colour can be very emotive, and often sets the scene for an event by creating the correct atmosphere. The same colour can be used to represent different emotions and events: for example blue celebrates the birth of a baby boy, and sapphire blue a forty-fifth wedding anniversary; red can represent love, Valentine's Day, Christmas, lust and danger; while yellow symbolizes sunshine, happiness and spring.

Colour can represent different emotions to different cultures: thus in China, red is for luck, while in India it signifies purity and is often used in wedding outfits. In Thailand the colour purple is associated with mourning and is not used for weddings. Blue in China means immortality, while in the Middle East it is considered to be a protective colour. The

LEFT: Hand-tied design: an example of split complementary colour harmony using red/violet, yellow and green.

Colour association – a textured cushion with pink flowers suitable for a girl/woman.

Colour association – a textured cushion more suitable for a boy/man, with the use of blue highlighted by cheerful yellow flowers.

colour orange is significant for Buddhist monks, who wear orange as a sign of their striving for enlightenment, while in Holland it symbolizes the Dutch royal family – on the Queen's birthday everyone wears orange.

Understanding the Colour Wheel

To understand colour it is important to study and understand the colour wheel. There are twelve colours on the colour wheel, classified as primary, secondary and tertiary colours; these may be identified as follows:

Primary colours: Red, yellow and blue. These colours cannot be created by mixing any other colours.
Secondary colours: Orange, green and violet. These colours are created by mixing certain primary colours in equal measure:
- red and yellow to create orange
- yellow and blue to create green
- blue and red to create violet

The colour wheel.
Key: Y = yellow, Y/O = yellow/orange, O = orange, R/O = red/orange, R = red, R/V = red/violet, V = violet, B/V = blue/violet, B = blue, B/G = blue/green, G = green, Y/G = yellow/green.

Tertiary colours: Yellow-green, blue-green, blue-violet, red-violet, red-orange, yellow-orange. These colours are created by mixing one primary and the adjacent secondary in equal measure:

- yellow and green to create yellow-green
- green and blue to create blue-green
- blue and violet to create blue-violet
- violet and red to create red-violet
- red and orange to create red-orange
- orange and yellow to create yellow-orange

(Note that the primary colour is always listed first when writing down tertiary colours, which are often depicted by initials only.)

A segment of the colour wheel showing colour modification:
hue + black = shade   hue + grey = tone
hue + white = tint

MODIFYING COLOURS
These colours can then be modified by adding white, grey or black:

- A colour with no modification is known as a 'hue'
- A hue with an equal amount of white added is known as a 'tint'
- A hue with an equal amount of grey added is known as a 'tone'
- A hue with an equal amount of black added is known as a 'shade'

Take green as an example of such modification:
- Green – colour with no modification (hue)
- Mint – green plus white (tint)
- Sage – green plus grey (tone)
- Bottle green – green with black (shade)

NEUTRAL COLOURS
In addition to the twelve colours and their modifications there are three colours that are regarded as neutral: black, grey and white. This group of colours is called 'achromatic'. (For the florist, green can be regarded as a neutral colour as all stems and foliages are green.)

COLOUR PROPERTIES
Certain colours are said to 'recede' from the eye of the viewer – blues through to violet – and others to 'advance' towards him – reds through to yellow. Blues and violets, the receding colours, can therefore be used to create space and depth in a design, and reds and yellows, the advancing colours, to give it more impact. Blues and violets are also colours that can evoke the sensation of something cold and refreshing, and reds and yellows the sensation of something warm and cosy. Luminosity is another significant property of certain colours, because luminous colours show up more than others, and it is important to be aware of this propensity when choosing flowers for, say, a large hall or a dark room. White is the most dominantly luminous colour, followed by yellow; the least luminous is violet. In addition most colours with a tint have a luminous property to them.

Colour Harmonies
'Colour harmony' is the phrase used to explain the relationship between colours and their position around the colour wheel. A florist is concerned with nine different harmonies and their impact, and these are explained in turn below.

MONOCHROMATIC COLOUR

HARMONY
'Mono' means one, and 'monochromatic' describes the use of any combination of hue, tint, tone or shade associated with one colour only, thereby creating a very subtle effect. The example pictured uses red/violet.

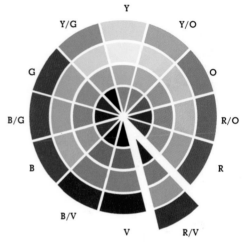

An example of monochromatic colours, where any combination of hue, tint, tone and shade of one colour is used – in this case red/violet.

Hand-tied design: an example of monochromatic harmony using red/violet.

POLYCHROMATIC COLOUR HARMONY

Polychromatic describes an assortment of colours, created from a combination of hues, tints, tones and/or shades. This creates a chaotic, jolly feel, although the effect can be confusing if only hues are used. The example pictured uses orange, yellow/orange, orange, and blue, blue/green, green.

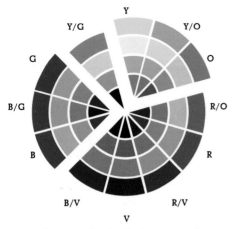

An example of polychromatic colours, where any combination of hue, tint, tone and shade of assorted colours is used – in this case yellow, yellow/orange, orange; blue, blue/green and green.

Hand-tied design: an example of polychromatic colour harmony.

ANALOGOUS COLOUR HARMONY

Analogous harmony is a subtle colour harmony created by using three to four colours with a combination of hues, tints, tones and/or shades (including one primary colour) that lie next to each other on the colour wheel. The example pictured uses yellow, yellow/orange, orange, red/orange.

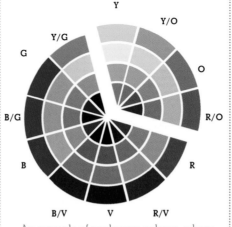

An example of analogous colours, where three to four colours that lie next to each other are used.

Hand-tied design: an example of analogous colour harmony using yellow, yellow/orange, orange and red/orange.

COMPLEMENTARY COLOUR HARMONY

Complementary harmony describes the combination of any of the hues, tints, tones and/or shades of colour that lie exactly opposite each other on the wheel – for example red and green – giving a vibrant effect. This colour harmony has maximum impact if hues only are used, with both a receding and an advancing colour in one palette. Think of holly at Christmas time, with the vibrant red berries set against the shiny green leaves. The example pictured uses red and green.

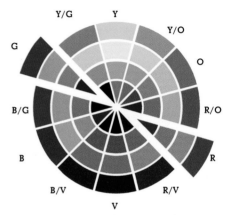

An example of complementary colours, where opposite colours in any combination of tint, tone, shade or hue are used – in this case red and green.

Hand-tied design: an example of complementary colour harmony using red and green.

SPLIT COMPLEMENTARY COLOUR HARMONY

Split complementary harmony consists of any combination of hues, tints, tones and/or shades of a colour on the wheel, and the colours that lie on each side of its complementary colour. The example pictured uses green, yellow, and red/violet.

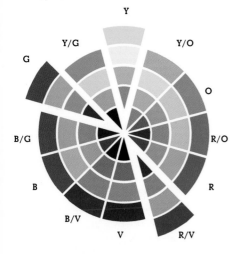

An example of split complementary colours, where any combination of tints, tones, shades or hues of a colour on the wheel, and the colours that lie on each side of its complementary colour, are used – in this case green, yellow, and red/violet.

Hand-tied design: an example of split complementary colour harmony using green, yellow, and red/violet.

NEAR COMPLEMENTARY COLOUR HARMONY

Near complementary harmony consists of a colour on the wheel, and one of the colours that lies beside its complementary colour. Any combination of hues, tints, tones and/or shades associated with these colours can be used. The example pictured uses pink (the tint of red) and yellow/green.

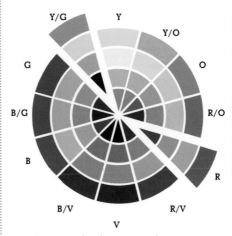

An example of near complementary colours, where any combination of tints, tones, shades or hues of a colour on the wheel, and one of the colours that lies beside its complementary colour, are used – in this case red and yellow/green.

Hand-tied design: an example of near complementary colour harmony using red (in this case pink with a tint of red) and yellow/green.

CONTRASTING COLOUR HARMONY

Contrasting harmony consists of any combination of hues, tints, tones and/or shades of colours that have no generic link (eg. primary colours); up to three colours can be used. The example pictured uses blue and yellow.

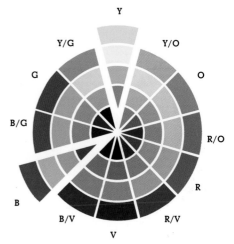

An example of contrasting colours, where any combination of tints, tones, shades or hues of colours with no generic link is used – in this case yellow and blue.

Hand-tied design: an example of contrasting colour harmony using yellow and blue.

TRIADIC COLOUR HARMONY

'Tri' means three, and triadic harmony describes any combination of hues, tints, tones and shades of three colour segments that lie an equal distance apart on the colour wheel (every fourth segment). The example pictured uses orange, violet and green.

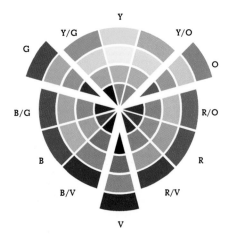

An example of triadic colours, where any combination of tints, tones, shades or hues of three colours equally spaced apart on the wheel is used – in this case orange, violet and green.

Hand-tied design: an example of triadic colour harmony using orange, violet and green.

TETRADIC COLOUR HARMONY

Tetradic harmony describes any combination of hues, tints, tones and shades of four colour segments that lie an equal distance apart on the colour wheel (every third segment). The example pictured uses blue/green, yellow, red/orange, violet.

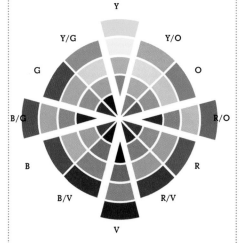

An example of tetradic colour harmony, where any combination of tints, tones, shades or hues of four colours equally spaced on the colour wheel is used – in this case blue/green, red/orange, yellow and violet.

Hand-tied design: an example of tetradic colour harmony using blue/green, red/orange, yellow and violet.

Form

The element of form can refer to both the outline shape of the design, and the shapes within it. The outline shape is concerned with a recognizable shape such as a circle, diamond, oval, asymmetric triangle, triangle or rectangle, to name but a few. Form is not just two-dimensional, but can also be three-dimensional; also the use of unusual forms can create considerable impact and visual interest – strelizlia (bird of Paradise) and fatsia japonica are fine examples of this.

Once the outline shape is determined, it is important to consider carefully the shape or form within the design. These shapes or forms can be divided in the main into three different types, known in floristry as point, line and transitional form.

This hand-tied floral display shows many different forms.

Point (or round) form: This is the strongest and most dominant form, and a limited use of this type of form is essential, otherwise the design becomes chaotic. Flowers that create a strong feeling of point form are gerberas, sunflowers, roses and carnations. These points are designed to attract the eye, and the most significant point within a design is known as the focal point, designed as a place for the eye to rest.

Line form: Materials that have line help to establish lines of sight in a design, and create height, width and direction in a floral display. They can have impact in linear and modern designs. Materials that achieve this effect include liatris, willow and exposed stems.

Transitional form: Typically this form is evoked by half-opened shapes such as foliages and half-opened flowers. In traditional designs transitional shapes are used to hide stems, and to give outline and dimension to shapes. Modern designs have little use for this form.

Space

Space is not always easy to visualize as a positive quality in a design, nevertheless it is an important design consideration that is often overlooked. There are two types of space:

• Positive space is the area occupied by the plant material in the design, which makes an imaginary outline that is part of the completed overall concept.
• Negative space is the shape or shapes that are created between the solid material shapes – that is, where there is no plant material within a design; this allows the eye some respite as it moves from one positive form to the next within the design.

It is important to appreciate that some space around each flower gives individual forms significance and allows the form of each flower to be seen: if the flowers are tightly packed throughout the design they will look cramped and uncomfortable. In modern and abstract designs, negative space is a major feature that is used to balance the solid area. The shape of the space is often determined by manipulating leaves and the use of caging techniques. Space is the counterfoil to solid, and without space there is no form; furthermore it can be used in various ways within and around floral designs, and even

An arrangement showing the use of both positive and negative space.

beneath the container to give a sense of lightness to the design and to prevent the arrangement looking too heavy. It can add variety, particularly in traditional designs, and in a design where there is a concentration of dense materials in, for instance, the focal area, slender materials

that are identified by the space between them can be used most effectively at the extremities of the display in order to create balance in the design. Space around the design should also be taken into consideration – for example, placing a floral design in a niche enhances the overall impact.

Space can be used as an illusion, to trick the eye into seeing depth where there is none, adding to the impression of space. Good use of space can appear to make the design look larger, thus saving money but looking better value to the customer.

Line

Line is easiest to understand if it is considered in two categories: firstly as the outline of your design, and secondly as the lines and accent lines within your design. The first relates to the outline of an arrangement, which can be vertical, horizontal, curved, triangular. The second category is the line within a floral design that gives it life and movement: it leads the eye along a definite path in the flower arrangement, which can be slow or swift, gentle or exciting. The line direction of the plant material used will help to determine the emotional impact of the display: thus thin, spike-like material gives a swift, dramatic line, while gently curving material gives elegance and softness, and broad material suggests slow movement. Equally line direction can express various feelings: thus vertical lines suggest strength and power, while horizontal lines seem more peaceful, implying calmness and tranquillity. Diagonal lines, on the other hand, express uncertainty, motion and excitement, whereas curved lines suggest motion in a more relaxed and graceful way.

Line can be actual, or it can be implied. Actual lines are plain to see, and the eye travels easily from one place to another because it is following an existing line – for example the lines produced by the stem of a flower, or by similar flowers placed in a line: these are real lines, and our eye follows them easily. Actual line forms the structure for a design: it can give it distinction and importance, providing shape and also a pathway for the eye to

An arrangement showing the use of both actual and implied line.

follow throughout an arrangement. Implied line also provides a pathway for the eye to follow, but no line actually exists. These lines can be created visually using similar flowers and elements, where the repetition of either colour or flowers can create implied lines. The direction of these different lines serves to lead the eye from one focal point to another.

The Principles of Design

If the 'elements' are the building blocks of good design, then the 'principles' are the 'cement' that holds them together – or if the elements are the ingredients for a recipe, then the principles are the method. There are seven principles of design: dominance, proportion, harmony, balance, contrast, scale and rhythm. An easy mnemonic by which to remember them is: Debbie Pedals Her Bike Carrying Scarlet Roses.

Dominance

Dominance in a design is achieved through the use of materials that grab the attention, however it is essential to use such materials carefully if the design is to be interesting but not 'over the top' in stimulating the senses. This principle can be achieved by:

- the strong use of colour, for example by selecting primary colours
- the interesting use of unusual textures such as the artichoke
- using large forms such as the helianthus (sunflower)
- the use of unusual forms such as the strelitzia (bird of paradise)
- the use of enclosed space – for instance manipulating looped grasses to create a cage
- using a mass of one material only

In modern design work there is an increased use of dominance, often with more than one focal point as compared to traditional designs where there is only one focal point.

Dominance is achieved in this design by using the round form and primary yellow of the gerbera.

This design is successful because it is constructed to the correct proportions.

Harmony: Careful consideration of the elements and principles of design have brought together soft colours and forms to create a basket eminently suitable for the birth of a baby girl.

Proportion

The principle of proportion refers to the construction of the design – in floristry terms this means the number or quantity of flowers and foliages used within a design in relation to each other. Satisfactory proportions can be achieved by applying mathematical dimensions, such as one third to two thirds: thus in a hostess bouquet one third of the material would lie below the tying point, and two thirds above, the two-third part of the design becoming the more dominant proportion (equal proportions are visually boring on the eye).

Proportions can also apply to colour, texture and form.

In advanced modern designs the classic European proportions of three, five and eight can apply.

Harmony

The principle of harmony is achieved if consideration is given to all the elements and principles, working them together to create one unified design that is fit for the purpose for which it is intended. What is meant by 'fit for purpose'? If pink flowers are suitable for the birth of a baby girl, would you arrange them in a square, black container? Better a container of a more feminine colour – maybe a tint of pink – and a softer shape.

The same consideration should apply to the location of a design – thus a modern-style design in a funky metal container would strike an inharmonious chord if placed in a period house.

The ultimate goal for any florist is to create a design that just feels and looks good in its final placement: then you know that you have achieved a harmonious result.

Balance

The florist is concerned with both actual and visual balance:

• Actual balance is achieved by the stability of the design. Thus the

An arrangement showing both actual balance – the candelabra and candles have not fallen over – and visual balance, achieved by the equal placement throughout of the white flowers.

Hand-tied design demonstrating sharp contrasts in texture, form and colour.

materials in a pedestal should be carefully placed so that their weight is evenly distributed and the pedestal is not at risk of toppling over; funeral designs in foam should not be over-soaked, when they might become too heavy to carry safely; wired work should have balance; buttonholes and corsages should be evenly balanced so they don't tip forwards when worn; and bridal bouquets when held should not be of uneven weight, but should feel balanced in the hand.

• Visual balance is achieved by a design looking balanced; this can be achieved by imagining a vertical axis through the middle of a design with an equal amount of material on each side (not necessarily the same). This can also be achieved by using an equal placement of colour throughout; an even use of textures and of form; small materials on the outer edges of the design; and darker colours in the middle. This does

not mean that every successful design must always be symmetrical: successful asymmetrical designs can be achieved still by using an equal weight of colour, texture or materials on each side of the imaginary axis. (Remember that dark colours, point forms, enclosed spaces and shiny textures have a strong eye pull, so use these in moderation.)

Contrast

The principle of contrast is best explained by the comparison of unlike or opposite qualities. This can be achieved in a variety of ways, including the use of colours, the size and texture of materials, and horizontal versus vertical placements within the design. Modern designs rely on the effective use of contrast to ensure they remain interesting – although in excess contrast can be distracting and the design will no longer retain its visual balance. Note that the use of contrast in traditional

designs is generally a more muted affair.

Contrast of form can be achieved by using more than one type of shaped material within a design, such as Alchemilla mollis, which has a small, fluffy form, with gerberas which have large, round points.

Contrast of colour is achieved by using different hues, tints, tones or shades within a design – so even a monochromatic design can achieve this; and always remember that to create impact, one colour should dominate (in the case of monochromatic the tint could be used in larger amounts).

Contrast in texture can be achieved by mixing smooth with rough materials.

Scale

The principles of scale and proportion are often confused by the trainee florist, but both are important and it is essential to understand the difference between them. Scale is concerned with the correct size of materials in relation to each other, and of the finished design in its final placement: for example, is the design to be worn like a buttonhole – are the materials of an appropriate size to be worn (not too large or too small in relation to the customer)? Is the container the correct size and scale for the chosen materials? If there are accessories such as butterflies to be included in the design, do they look in scale to the chosen flowers? Or if the design is to be placed in a fireplace hearth or church, is it the right height and width to look suitable in its final position? Estimating the correct scale for a large venue is always difficult when constructing the design in a workshop, so on a site visit before you even begin constructing your design it is advisable to measure the final placement area and make notes regarding the size and proportions that will be required, so that on delivery of the

finished design it does not look too small or out of scale.

Rhythm

Without the principle of rhythm a design can appear 'flat' and uninteresting. A good design appears to be imbued with a certain amount of animation even though the materials are still. Rhythm can be achieved by way of:

- radiation – where materials radiate from a focal point; this is especially true of traditional designs

- variation – of line, form and colour, creating lines of sight for the eye to follow
- graduation – where materials are graduated in size and colour, with smaller buds or lighter colours on the outside of a design, and larger heads and darker colours in the middle
- repetition – where colour, line and form is repeated; form can also be repeated in the choice of container in the arrangement – as, for example, round gerberas in a round container.

The size of the materials and the overall size of the design are both in perfect scale for the position of this display on the top of the cake.

Rhythm is achieved in this design by the repetition of colour and form, and the way the flowers radiate from the centre.

Chapter 4
Tied Designs

Tied designs offer the florist a range of design ideas and the customer a range of price points, from budget prices with a few stems to expensive luxury designs with many stems or a few choice stems. These designs also offer the customer a variety of outcomes: pre-made designs that only need placing in a vase, pre-made designs that are created and delivered in water, or cut flowers that customers can select for themselves and use to create their own vase designs or arrangements. Tied designs are suitable for many occasions: the peak periods of Mother's Day and Valentine's Day, birthdays, the birth of a baby, an engagement, get well gifts, to name but a few. In addition, compact tied designs can be suitable for wedding bouquets, and tied sheaf designs suitable for funeral orders.

....

Gift Wrapping Cut Flowers and Foliages

All designs require gift wrap: not only does it enhance the presentation and the perceived value of the floral display, it also protects it from adverse weather and makes transportation easier. 'PPT' best describes this: Presentation, Protection, Transportation.

There is a wide range of exciting gift-wrap products for the florist to use, with products coming on to the market all the time, so take time to master the different techniques.

Presentation styles can differ and are subject to trends: for example, brown paper and raffia appeal to the eco-friendly

LEFT: Tropical flowers make a limited hand-tied design.

customer, so keep your presentation skills up to date with these trends.

All tied flowers will need appropriate flower food (see Chapter 2) and care instructions so the customer can gain the very best from their cut flower, tied designs. It is also important to advise customers as to the best way to transport their floral designs so they get them home safely. Priorities are to keep the design secure, and to avoid any prolonged time in a vehicle – too hot and the flower material will wilt, too cold and it will perish.

The following section describes the different techniques and materials used by the florist to gift wrap cut flowers and foliages, both singly and in a variety of designs.

Single Flower Cellophane Wrapped

MATERIALS
Fresh flowers and foliages
One Rosa 'Memory Lane'
Three Liriope muscari (lily grass)

Sundries
One plastic phial
Cellophane
Ribbon
Clear tape
Flower envelope/card/flower food
Florist's scissors

SUITABILITY
A single flower offers a budget purchase or an individual luxury purchase: for example on Valentine's Day a single red Rosa or orchid. It is important to keep the stem at its full length because the customer pays for the length of stem in the flower price.

Storage (florist)
Store upright so that the water level in the phial covers the stem end.

Care (customer)
Re-cut the stem 2.5cm (1in) from the base. Place it in a suitable vase with fresh tepid water and diluted flower food. Replace the water and re-cut the stem every three days, adding fresh flower food as necessary. Keep out of direct sunlight, and away from draughts and fresh fruit. Avoid leaving it in the car for prolonged periods because it will be vulnerable to the fluctuating temperature (over the Valentine's Day period the car seems to be a favourite 'hiding place', but often the temperature is too cold, killing the Rosa before it is given to the recipient).

GIFT-WRAP METHOD
1. Lay the stem diagonally on the cellophane, and cut the cellophane so that it fits the length of the individual stem – never cut the stem to fit the cellophane because often the price of the flower is higher if the stem is longer (this reflects particular care during the growing procedure). Cut the stem at an acute angle (this will increase the surface area of the stem available to water and therefore maximize hydration), fill a plastic phial with water, put the lid on, and then insert the Rosa and grass through the lid.

2. Fold up the excess cellophane at the bottom, then fold over one side of the cellophane and then the other, creating a cone, and secure with tape.

1. Cut the cellophane.

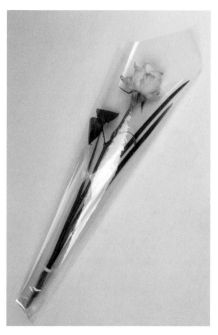

2. Fold the cellophane over the stem...

To attach either a single or a double
bow securely on to any design: cut the
ribbon that goes around the centre of
the bow extra long so that you can tie
the bow onto the design and then
once above the bow and once below
it; this will anchor it firmly.

Step one of tying a single bow...

3. Add a double bow above the phial –
   this secures the stem in the cellophane
   and adds an attractive presentation
   detail to the gift wrap. Add a sachet of
   flower food and a care card.

Any individual stem can be elegantly gift
wrapped; purpose-made flower boxes can
also be used for this purpose instead of
cellophane.

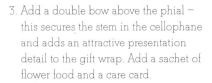

3. ...and finish off with a double bow.

Step two: tying around the centre
to secure it...

Tying a double bow – finish off as step
two of a single bow.

Bouquet Cone Wrapped with Craft Paper

MATERIALS
Fresh flowers and foliages
Ten Tulipa

Sundries
Craft paper
Coloured tissue paper
Ribbon
Clear tape
Flower envelope/card/flower food
Florist's scissors

SUITABILITY
This bouquet is suitable for a low budget impulse buy or gift – for a birthday, Mother's Day, a cheer up/get well gift or a personal present. It is a quick, easy and cheap gift wrap for the florist to create – and it can be made even cheaper by leaving out the tissue paper finish and the bow. It is important to keep the stems at their full length because the customer pays for the length of stem in the individual flower price.

Storage (florist)
When a cone is to be collected, wrap it ready, but expose the stems – leave them in water with flower food, and out of direct sunlight (due to the phototropic response of Tulipas – they move to the light). Cover the stems when delivery is imminent. If the purchase is to be immediate there is no need for storage.

Care (customer)
Re-cut the stems 2.5cm (1in) from the base. Place the bouquet in a suitable vase with fresh tepid water and diluted flower food for bulb flowers (amend the type of flower food depending on the flowers). Replace the water and re-cut the stems every three days, adding fresh flower food as necessary. Keep out of direct sunlight, and away from draughts and fresh fruit.

GIFT-WRAP METHOD
With stems exposed:
1. Cut the craft paper and tissue in a square. Fold it over to make a triangle that does not quite line up (so there are two peaks) so that the inner sandwich of tissue is on show. Lay the flowers on the paper so that the stems are below the folded edge.

2. Roll one side of the triangle under the stems...

3. ...and then keep rolling the flowers until the wrap is all the way round them; fasten with clear tape. You could add a double polyribbon bow (optional), tying the middle of the bow all the way round the wrap, then tying once above and once below the bow for security. You could also add a sachet of flower food, a care card and a shop sticker (also optional).

1. Cut the paper and lay the flowers on it...

2. Roll the paper over...

3. ...and finish the gift wrap with a bow.

With stems concealed:

1. Cut a square of craft and tissue paper as before (see Stems exposed, Step 1), then fold over the tissue to create a triangle that has two top peaks. Lay the flowers on the paper, keeping the wet

1. Lay the flowers on the pre-cut paper.

3. Fasten the wrap.

stem ends off the tissue.

2. Roll one side of the wrapping paper triangle under the stems...

2. Roll one side of the paper under the stems...

4. Finish the gift wrap with a bow.

3. ...then keep rolling the bouquet until the wrap is all the way round it, and fasten with clear tape. Fold the excess paper at the bottom of cone to the back, and fasten with tape.

4. You could add a double bow, also a sachet of flower food and a care card (these are optional).

Bouquet Cone Wrapped with Cellophane and Tissue

MATERIALS
Fresh flowers and foliages
Five Alchemilla mollis
Four Paeonia 'Sarah Bernhardt'

Sundries
Cellophane
Coloured tissue paper
Ribbon
Clear tape
Flower envelope/card/flower food
Florist's scissors

SUITABILITY
A front-facing, flat design, this versatile form of presentation is suitable for a few choice stems of chosen flowers/foliage. With such a wide range of ribbons and cellophane to choose from, many different presentation styles are possible, from traditional to contemporary. This bouquet is suitable for an impulse buy or a small gift – for a birthday, Mother's Day, a cheer up/get well gift, a personal present. This a quick, easy and cheap gift wrap for the florist to make.

It is important to keep the stems at their full length because the customer pays for the length of stem in the individual flower price.

Storage (florist)
This type of bouquet is normally gift wrapped in front of the customer, so no

storage is required. However, if it is a pre-ordered gift wrap, leave the bottom unwrapped and put the stems in water – keep it upright, and store in a dark, cool area.

Care (customer)

Re-cut the stems 2.5cm (1in) from the base. Place the flowers in a suitable vase with fresh tepid water and diluted flower food. Replace the water and re-cut the stems every three days, adding fresh flower food as necessary. Keep out of direct sunlight, and away from draughts and fresh fruit.

GIFT-WRAP METHOD

1. Cut a rectangle of cellophane, then fold a piece of tissue to resemble a 'kite' shape so that it fits within the outside edge of the cut cellophane. Create a pleasing outline shape with the stems, using the top edge of the gift wrap as a guide. Do not allow the flower heads to extend outside this as the gift wrap will protect them from damage and environmental conditions.

2. Arrange the focal flowers – in this case the Paeonia – on the paper to create visual balance: if the number of stems allows, stems on the right hand side can be laid at an angle under the binding point, and stems on the left hand side laid on top of the binding point, ie. the point where the string will eventually be tied. Make sure that all the stems are long enough to be secured at the binding point.

3. Fold one side of the cellophane over the stems and then the other, and secure with clear sticky tape. The bottom of the cone can be left open, or sealed by folding the excess cellophane to the back of the cone; fasten as required.

4. Attach a polyribbon or raffia bow over the binding point, and ensure that all

1. Cut out the cellophane and place the first flowers on it.

2. Arrange the rest of the flowers.

3. Fold over the cellophane...

4. ... and secure with a double bow.

5. The completed design.

the stems are secure so that when the bouquet is picked up none of the stems slides out.

5. Check that all is secure. Finally attach an appropriate flower food sachet, also a gift card and envelope, and a company sticker (optional).

The flowers chosen will give this bouquet either a contemporary or a traditional feel; for maximum effect a bold focal flower should be used, such as Rosa, Helianthus, Heliconia, Hippeastrum, Cymbidium orchid.

Flat Pack using Cellophane
MATERIALS
Fresh flowers and foliages
½ bunch Eucalyptus cinerea
Four Ruscus hypophyllum
Two Fatsia japonica

Eight Tulipa 'Golden Parade'
Four Gerbera 'Dino'
Three Phlox 'Miss Fiona'
Three Delphinium 'Sydney Purple'
Six Alchemilla

Sundries
Cellophane
Ribbon
Clear tape
Flower envelope/card/flower food
Florist's scissors, secateurs

SUITABILITY
A front-facing, flat design, this form of presentation is suitable for multiple stems of chosen flowers/foliage. With the wide range of choice of ribbons and cellophanes available, many different presentation styles are possible, from the traditional to the contemporary. It is important to keep the stems at their full length because the customer pays for the length of stem in the individual flower price.

This design is ideal for the customer who wishes to arrange the cut flowers themselves, offering more variety to those who enjoy working with flowers. A flat pack design is suitable for a gift for many occasions, for young or old, man or woman. It is suitable for a funeral, and is a good option for cremation ceremonies, as the flowers can be taken home or given away afterwards.

Storage (florist)
If the customer is collecting the flat pack later, gift wrap the flowers leaving the stem ends unwrapped, and put them in water with flower food; due to the phototropic response of the Tulipas (they move to the light) make sure the design is shielded from direct sunlight. When the customer arrives to collect the design, or it is to be delivered, wrap up the stems. (If the flowers are bought immediately there is no need for these storage measures.)

Care (customer)
Re-cut the stems 2.5cm (1in) from the base. Place the bouquet in a suitable vase with fresh tepid water and diluted flower food suitable for bulb flowers. Replace the water and re-cut the stems every three days, adding fresh flower food as necessary. Place the design away from direct sunlight, and away from draughts and fresh fruit.

GIFT-WRAP METHOD
1. Using the main foliages, in this case Eucalyptus cinerea, form a pointed outline shape (the aim is to create a triangular outline). Throughout when creating this design, position all centrally placed stems straight, all stems angled to the right-hand side of the design underneath these at the binding point (where the design will be tied), and all stems angled to the left-hand side over these at the binding point. Positioning the stems in this manner creates a spiralled effect, and when the design is tied the angle of the stems does not move.

2. Place the focal flowers Gerbera staggered down the middle, interspersed with Alchemilla and foliages to help build up the profile.

3. Next add the Delphinium and half the Ruscus angled to the right side, layering the flowers so that each individual bloom can be seen, and sliding the stems under the central flowers at the binding point. Next add the Phlox on the other side, layering them with the remaining Ruscus and laying the stems over the central flowers at the binding point. Try to create a balance of colour on both sides.

4. Add the shorter Tulipa stems across the centre, following the same technique: stems to the right under the straight stems at the binding point, some straight stems, stems to the left over the

1. Form outline shape

2. Arrange the focal flowers in a staggered line down the centre.

3. Add the taller flowers and foliage to each side...

4. ...and the shorter flowers to each side lower down.

5. Tie at the binding point.

6. Cut the cellophane, fold the sides over the design and staple.

7. Attach the bow.

8. The finished, gift-wrapped design.

straight stems at the binding point;
layer these with the shorter stems of the
foliage Fatsia japonica.

5. Tie securely with string, and then secure
the string by binding with 12mm pot
tape.

6. Cut the cellophane large enough to
completely envelop the tied design,
ensuring there is enough to gather at
the binding point without squashing
the flowers. Place the design flat on the
cellophane so the binding point is on
the bottom edge of the cellophane. Fold
the side edges of the cellophane over
the design and staple together.

7. Gather the lower edge together and
secure it with tape. You can choose
whether to cut a separate piece of
cellophane and cover the stems; if the
design is being collected later, leave it

upright in a bucket or vase of water and
wrap the stems later. Secure with a bow
finish.

8. Check that no materials are being
squashed by the cellophane, and that
all materials are securely fastened at the
binding point. Add a flower food sachet
and a gift card and envelope (optional).

Tied Bouquets

A favourite design comprises spiralled
stems that are tied and gift wrapped
and/or aqua packed (with its own
independent water vessel), or gift wrapped
in a vase. Depending on the flower choice,
this design is suitable for a wide range of
gift options – for the birth of a child, as a
get well present, for a birthday – and it is a
regular request for the peak times of

Valentine's Day or Mother's Day. The use of aqua packing means there is little maintenance for the recipient, and transporting the design is easy for the customer. These designs are ready to be placed in a vase of choice when the gift wrap is removed.

The main construction requirement for tied designs is that the stems spiral, which is achieved by placing all the stems at a 45-degree angle in the same direction. Without gift wrap the tied-design technique is suitable for bridal work, using compact flowers, normally with shorter stems. It is also increasingly requested for funeral work, as the design can be given away after the service and the flowers enjoyed by the new recipient.

Bouquet of Mixed Flowers, Aqua Packed

MATERIALS

Fresh flowers and foliages
Five Rosa 'Memory Lane'
Three Chrysanthemum 'Feeling Green'
Eight Veronica 'Dark Martje'
Eight Phlox
Eight Aspidistra
$^1/_2$ bunch Gaultheria shallon – tips
Twenty Ruscus hypophyllum

Sundries
Floristry scissors/secateurs
String, pot tape
Cellophane, green tissue
Ribbon
Flower pick/envelope/card/flower food
Optional gift bag

SUITABILITY

This is suitable as a gift for many occasions – for birthdays, as a get well, cheer up or thank you present, to celebrate an anniversary, the birth of a baby, retirement. This design is created in water so there is no need for the recipient to arrange these flowers. Because it can be viewed all the way round it can be placed on a table top

or coffee table of choice.

Storage (florist)

Store in a dark, cool area until delivery or collection; top up with water and flower food as required.

Care (customer)

Avoid placing the bouquet in direct sunlight, draughts, near fruit or in fluctuating temperatures. Keep the water topped up via the centre of the bouquet. Remove from the cellophane gift wrap after three days. Re-cut the stems 2.5cm (1in) from the base, and place the bouquet in a suitable vase with fresh, tepid water and diluted flower food. Replace the water and re-cut the stems every three days, adding fresh flower food as necessary.

METHOD

1. Prepare all the materials for tied use – defoliate all the stems that fall below the binding point, and create a core centre to spiral the other stems round. This is achieved by using a focal flower, Rosa, with foliage – for example three pieces of Ruscus.

2. Start to add the other materials, angling the flower heads towards you and the stems at a 45-degree angle; where you hold the bouquet will become the binding point. Work in threes to help keep the posy shape (even numbers of four will make it look square). Add the three Chrysanthemums at equal intervals.

3. Start to build up the design, adding in the heads at a 45-degree angle; you will notice that the stems below the binding point (where your hand is) will take on a spiral appearance.

4. Add the outer ring of flowers, evenly spaced, and wedge more foliages in between to maintain the spacing – always angling in these stems. Add

1. Create a centre core of a flower and foliage.

2. Add the three Chrysanthemums.

3. The stems start to spiral.

4. Add the outer ring of flowers.

5. Add the folded Aspidistra leaf collar.

6. Cut the stems.

7. Stand the bouquet upright.

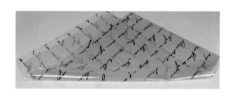

8. Lay out the outer gift-wrap collar.

9. Fold the first collar round the binding point.

10. Fold round the second collar.

11. Add the cellophane for the aqua packaging.

12. Carefully fill with water through the centre of the flowers.

cellophane around the stems, and hold them tightly around the original binding point – keep pulling the cellophane until it is taut across the bottom of the stems. Tie off the cellophane with string (this can be rather fiddly), positioning this tying point over the original binding point.

12. Tie on a bow, and then pour water carefully into the centre of the design: it will flow down through the flowers and into the vessel you have created with the cellophane.

13. For ease of transportation you can put the finished design into a purpose-made carry bag or purpose-made box vase (optional). Check that all the materials are free of damage, that all the stems are in water, and that the design is stable and will not fall over. Spray with water if the materials used allow. Add a care card, and appropriate flower food.

13. For ease of transport put the design into a purpose-made carry bag or box vase.

additional foliage as required to keep the outline. The photographed example has a ring of Rosa, Phlox and Veronica.

5. Finally add a collar of folded Aspidistra leaves. Tie all the stems at the binding point firmly with string.

6. Cut the spiralled stems by holding them firmly in one hand and then cutting right across them all with the other; the length of the stems from the binding point should be about half of the height of the design above the binding point.

7. Stand the bouquet upright, giving it a gentle tap to help it settle – the spiralled stems will support the bouquet in a vertical position.

8. The design is ready to collar gift wrap: cut two pieces of cellophane to fit the rectangular coloured tissue, and fold over.

9. Fold the first collar round the base of the design, again using the tied binding point as a guide; secure with sticky tape.

10. Fold the second collar, starting at the widest part in the 'gap' of the first fold around either side, and secure.

11. For the aqua packing (which can be optional), cut a double square of cellophane – the double layer will help prevent thorns or sharp stems sticking through the bottom – and then place the bouquet upright in the middle of the squares. Pull up the edges of the

Bouquet, Grouped Textured

MATERIALS
Fresh flowers and foliages
Nine small Rosa 'Marie-Claire'
Five Hypericum 'Coco'
Three Leucospermum 'Tango'
Two Chrysanthemum 'Kermit'
Three Leucadendron 'Goldstrike'
Eight Ruscus hypophyllum
Ten Aspidistra

Sundries
Craft paper/tissue
Ribbon
String/pot tape
Flower pick/envelope/card/flower food
Florist's knife and scissors, and secateurs
Leafshine

SUITABILITY
A grouped textured design is a contemporary variation of the hand-tie

design, but still suitable for many occasions – for birthdays, as a get well, cheer you up or thank you present, or to celebrate an anniversary, or retirement. The choice of a bold-coloured flower and the use of contrasting, unusual textures creates a very modern design that can be recreated in different profiles – the photographed example is a posy style, but the design can be made front-facing. This style of design is suitable for both genders and all ages.

This design can be placed straightaway in the vase of choice, so there is no need for the recipient to arrange the flowers. A smaller version of this design could be used for bridal work.

Storage (florist)
Store in a dark, cool area and keep the stems in water until delivery or collection. This design can be aqua packed or sold with a vase.

Care (customer)
Keep away from direct sunlight, draughts and fruit, and avoid fluctuating temperatures. Keep the water topped up via the centre of the bouquet. Re-cut the stems 2.5cm (1in) from the base, and place the bouquet in a suitable vase with fresh tepid water and diluted flower food.

Replace the water and re-cut the stems every three days, adding fresh flower food as necessary.

METHOD
1. Prepare all the materials for tied use by defoliating all the stems below the binding point. Fold over and staple securely the Aspidistra leaves – these will be used as a collar in the later stages of the design, and also within it to create contrasts of texture; spray them with leafshine (observing the manufacturer's instructions regarding ventilation).

Start to tie the design together by using the most dominant of your textured materials Leucospermum at the centre; then add groups of materials, arranging them so they spiral round the Leucospermum (spiralling is achieved by angling the flowers and foliage at 45°) – choose contrasting textures such as the shiny small-leaved Ruscus against the spiky Leucospermum, and the matt oval leaves of the Leucadendron 'Goldstrike'.

2. Continue with this process of adding groups of like-textured materials to create maximum texture opposites, being careful to maintain a visual balance of colour and the posy outline shape.

3. To finish this design add a collar of folded Aspidistra leaves.

4. Tie off firmly using string, binding over this with 12mm pot tape for added security.

5. Hold the stems firmly with one hand

1a. Create a centre core of flowers, starting with the focal area.

1b. Where you hold the design will become the finished binding point.

2. Build up a posy outline with groups of materials.

3. Add a folded aspidistra leaf collar.

4. Tie firmly with string.

5. Cut the stems, then stand the bouquet upright to check for balance.

below the binding point, and cut straight across them with the other – the length of the stems below the binding point should be half the height of the design above the binding point.

6. Gift wrap by cutting two squares of craft paper with matching coloured tissue paper to fit, folding this over to create two triangles (see Cone-wrapped gift-wrap method, Exposed stems, above), then folding in the ends of the triangle.

7. Wrap each prepared craft paper round the base of the design, and secure at the binding point with clear tape; then fold over the tips of the triangle to create a contemporary gift wrap.

Try and choose flowers with the same lifespan as each other, and with a selection of textural interest and colour dominance. See the texture guide in Chapter 3.

6. Cut and fold both tissue and craft paper to create collars.

7. Secure both collars round the base of the flowers.

Bouquet in a Self-Made Frame (Version 1)

There are many different variations of frame that can be either shop bought or constructed; these frames create a collar effect around a selection of tied flowers and foliages. This is one idea for a self-constructed frame.

MATERIALS
Fresh flowers and foliages
Seven Papaver (poppy)
Three Rosa 'Avalanche Sorbet'
Three Paeonia 'Sarah Bernhardt'
Four Celosia 'Bombay Pink'
Seven Pittosporum tobira
Three Ruscus hypophyllum
Eight Origanum (oregano) 'Rose Charm'

Sundries
Door wreath frame 30cm in diameter
120mm wires, floral tape
Plastic mesh gift wrap
String/pot tape
Flower pick/envelope/ card/flower food
Florist's knife and scissors
Vase/coloured floral water

SUITABILITY
This design is an appropriate gift for many occasions – for birthdays, as a get well, cheer you up or thank you present, to celebrate an anniversary, the birth of a baby, retirement. It is designed either to be sold with a vase, or to be placed by the customer into a vase of their own. It can be viewed all the way round, so it can quite happily be placed on a table top or coffee table of choice.

Storage (florist)
As for the grouped textured design.

Care (customer)
As for the grouped textured design.

METHOD
1. Tape three 120mm wires, and attach them to the door-wreath frame (refer to Chapter 6 Weddings, Bridal Single Flower Design, for guidance on the frame construction). Using decorative wire, start to attach the mesh to the frame.

2. Continue to attach the mesh, gathering it into a pleasing profile and outline and taking care to obscure the frame. Complete the process of attachment until the whole frame is covered.

3. Prepare all the materials for tied use by defoliating all the stems that fall below the binding point. Insert the foliages so as to form a base into which to insert the flowers in the next stage; use the spiral technique as explained earlier in this chapter to secure the foliage.

4. Add the filler throughout the bouquet; in the photographed example it is Oregano. Now add groups of flowers by threading them into the foliage, angling the heads at 45 degrees to continue the spiral process. The groups of flowers need to be bold in shape or strongly coloured, such as Peonia, Rosa and Celosia.

5. Tie off the design with string, and bind pot tape over the string to secure it. Gather the stems together and cut them with secateurs. The length of the stems will vary depending on how the design is being presented – if aqua packing you will need to keep the stems long enough to gift wrap in this way. If the bouquet is going in a vase, cut the stems so that the frame sits nicely on the vase rim.

6. Check that all materials are free of damage, that all the stems are in water, and that the design is stable and will not fall over. Mist with water, as long as the materials are such that they will not be damaged.

1. Attach the mesh to the frame with decorated wire.

2. The finished frame.

3. Insert the foliages into the frame, spiralling the stems.

4. Insert the flowers in groups of similar colour and texture.

5. Cut the stems and stand the bouquet upright to check for balance.

6. Put the bouquet into the vase with coloured floral water.

ALTERNATIVE IDEAS
Use different waterproof materials to wire on to the door-wreath frame to create different versions of this concept – for example, floral-purpose organzas. Use a smaller frame to create a smaller posy which could then be used for a bride or bridesmaid. Attach fresh materials on to the frame, such as an ivy trail – see Chapter 6 Weddings for this design.

Bouquet in a Self-Made Frame (Version 2)

This design has a rather craft approach, with two collars of card cut to a desired shape and sandwiched together.

MATERIALS
Fresh flowers and foliages
Thirteen Equisetum grass (ten for the frame and three for the design)
Six Papaver (poppy)
Three Paeonia 'Sarah Bernhardt'
Four Celosia 'Bombay Pink'
Three Aspidistra leaves (folded)

Sundries
Card, cut into your desired shape (old flower boxes are suitable)
120mm wires, floral tape
String/ pot tape
Flower pick/ envelope/ card/ flower food
Florist's knife and scissors
Vase

1. Stick Equisetum grass on to pre-cut
card.

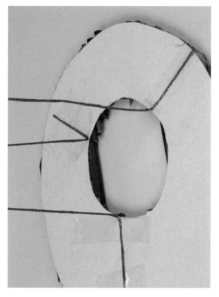

2. Stick on taped wires to make a handle.

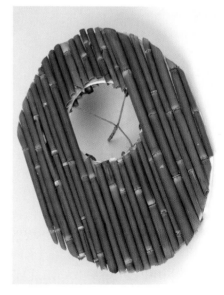

3. Sandwich both the cards together, and
tape the centre wires to make the handle.

SUITABILITY

A gift for many occasions – for birthdays,
as a get well gift, to cheer you up or as a
thank you, for an anniversary, the birth of a
baby, retirement. The use of a bold-
coloured flower choice or contrasting
unusual textures creates a very modern
design that can be recreated in different
profiles. This design is created to be either
sold with a vase or placed by the customer
into a vase of their own. As it can be
viewed all the way round it can be placed
on a table top or coffee table of choice.

Storage (florist)

As for the grouped textured design.

Care (customer)

As for the grouped textured design.

METHOD

1. Cut out two shapes of card – these
   need to be exactly the same. Cut out a
   hole in the middle, big enough to
   accommodate the materials used, but
   taking care that it is not too big as this
   would take more materials to fill it and

4. Insert groups of flowers into the frame,
spiralling the stems.

5. Continue to insert groups of flowers...

would thereby increase the cost to the
customer. Stick strips of double-sided
tape across one side of the card, then
remove the backing and place
Equisetum stems on to the sticky tape,

cutting them to size to fit the cardboard
frame. Repeat this process for the other
side of the frame.

2. Tape three 120mm wires, and bend

6. ...cutting the stems and then adding them to the vase.

and peonies for maximum contrast in texture and form. Prepare the materials for tied use by defoliating all the stems below the binding point. Start with the centre of the design, making a central core of stems in which to start spiralling the remainder. To improve the harmony, include some stems of Equisetum; here, each stem has been wired by threading a heavy 90mm wire through its centre so it can be manipulated into position more easily.

5. Continue to add in the stems until the centre of the frame is filled, being careful to keep the stems spiralled as you insert them into the frame.

6. Tie off the design with string, and secure it by binding with pot tape. Gather the stems together and cut with secateurs. The length of the stems will vary depending on how the design is being presented – if it is to be aqua packed, you will need to keep the stems long enough to gift wrap in this way; if it is going in a vase, cut them so that the frame sits nicely on the vase rim.

7. Check that all the materials are free of damage, that all the stems are in water, and that the design is stable and will not fall over. Mist with water, as long as the materials are such that they will not be damaged if you do so.

ALTERNATIVE IDEAS
Many different looks can be achieved using card in this way as a collar. Cover the collar with ribbon, autumn leaves, fabric, wool, to name but a few, to create a variety of techniques.

Bouquet in a Bought, Ready-made Frame

Frames are available from your local wholesaler: they are normally purchased in a small bale, with quantities varying from

and attach them to the frame.

3. Sandwich them between the other covered piece of card, and stick them together. Tape together the supporting wires to make a handle.

4. The frame has a contemporary feel to it, so the flower choice needs to reflect this: use bold textures and shapes next to each other to create contrast and visual interest – the example in the photograph uses poppy heads, Celosia

as few as five up to twenty-five or more. They are great to use over a peak period when time is of the essence – frame designs can reflect this, with heart-shaped ones in bright reds and hot pinks over Valentine's Day, and pastel-coloured flower-shaped ones for Mother's Day. You can also purchase seasonal frames suitable for Christmas, autumn, and so on.

MATERIALS
Fresh flowers and foliages
Four Paeonia 'Sarah Bernhardt'

Three Phlox 'Miss Fiona'
Five Alchemilla
Three Pittosporum tobira
Four Ruscus hypophyllum

Sundries
Pre-bought sisal frame
String/pot tape
Flower pick/envelope/card/flower food
Florist's knife and scissors
Vase

SUITABILITY
This is a gift for many occasions – birthdays, as a get well, cheer you up, thank you present, for an anniversary, the birth of a baby, retirement. It can be sold with a vase, or the customer can use a suitable vase of their own. Because it can be viewed all the way round it can be placed on a table top or coffee table of choice.

Storage (florist)
As for the grouped textured design.

Care (customer)
As for the grouped textured design.

METHOD
1. Use a bought frame. Prepare the materials for tied use by defoliating all the stems below the binding point. Insert the foliages to form a base, using the spiral technique as explained earlier in this chapter.

2. Add the filler flowers to the design, spiralling the materials as you insert them through the foliage base.

3. Insert one focal flower into the middle, and the other three round it. Next add the rest of the flowers. Tie off the design with string, and secure it by binding with pot tape. Gather the stems together and cut them with secateurs; the length of the stems will vary depending on how the design is being presented – if aqua packing you will need to keep the stems long enough to gift wrap in this way, if going in a vase, cut them so that the frame sits nicely on the vase rim.

4. Check that all the materials are free of damage, that all the stems are in water, and that the design is stable and will not fall over. Mist with water if the materials are appropriate to do so.

1. Add foliages to the pre-bought frame, spiralling the stems.

2. Add the filler flower Alchemilla throughout the design, spiralling the stems.

3. Add the flowers into the design ...

4. ... cutting the stems and then adding them to the vase.

Bouquet Limited Hand-tied

MATERIALS

Fresh flowers and foliages
Four Alphina
One Heliconia wagneriana
Three Heliconia 'Opal'
Three small Monstera
Two Palm
One Cordyline
Eight Rucus hypophyllum
Four Aspidistra

Sundries
Sisal wrap
Green willow and green decorative wire
Ribbon
String/pot tape
Flower pick/envelope/card/flower food
Florist's knife and scissors/secateurs

SUITABILITY
This is a long-lasting contemporary hand-tie design with limited floral materials; bold/unusual flowers are needed for

1. Construct the frame and add Cordyline as a centre core.

2. Add the centre flower Heliconia.

3. Add the Alphina, layering it with the foliage, and angling the stems behind the binding point.

4. Add the Opal, layering it with the foliage and angling the stems in front of the binding point.

5. Add the lower leaves.

6. Tie off securely with string.

7. Add sisal wrap around the binding point.

maximum effectiveness. It is suitable as a gift for many occasions – for birthdays, as a get well, cheer you up, thank you present, to celebrate an anniversary, the birth of a baby, retirement; being high impact and low maintenance it could also be used for corporate work, especially in a hot office or beauty-related business where the environment can be very hot. This design is tied ready for the customer to place in their vase of choice. It is constructed in a front-facing fashion so it should be placed on a sideboard, fire place or reception desk where it will only be viewed from one side.

Storage (florist)
Keep at room temperature (if using tropical flowers) until delivery or collection. Keep the stems in water.

Care (customer)
Avoid placing this design in direct sunlight, in a draught or near fruit, and protect from fluctuating temperatures. Replace the water and re-cut the stems every three days, adding fresh flower food as necessary.

METHOD

1. Construct a couple of small frames out of bright-coloured willow to give the design structure (this is optional – see Wiring Techniques in Chapter 6 for guidance). Prepare the materials for tied use by defoliating all the stems below the binding point.

2. Create a core of materials in the centre of the design – here, the main Heliconia in the middle is 'wedged' into place with Ruscus and folded aspidistra leaves.

3. Insert Alphina, creating a spiral by placing the stems behind. Layer the flowers so that each individual flower can be seen.

4. Insert the small Heliconia 'Opal' on the other side; this time the spiral is achieved by placing the stems in front, again layering the individual stems.

5. Add the plaited palms (see Leaf manipulation techniques) into the back of the design; balance these by adding folded aspidistra leaves. Lastly, add a couple of large, bold Monstera leaves, continuing to spiral the stems, at the base of the design.

6. Tie off the design with string and pot tape, then cut the stems.

7. To gift wrap, pressed sisal gift wrap has been wrapped round this design and fastened to the binding point. Finally, check that all materials are fastened securely and have not incurred any damage. Mist the design.

ALTERNATIVE IDEAS

Other bold flowers could be Helianthus (large sun flowers), Hippeastrum, a large stem of Cymbidium orchids, Kniphofia, Protea, Strelitiza (bird of paradise), Zantedeschia.

Threading

Threading beads or natural alternative Hypericum heads on to either grasses or thin flexi-cane can add distinctive lines throughout many styles of design work.

1. Coloured foam cubes are threaded alternately with Hypericum berries onto modelino-coloured cane (for details of this effect, see the coloured foam design in Chapter 5 Arrangements).

2. Thread Hypericum berries onto Ficinea facicularis (flexi-grass) (for details of this effect, see Loose, open-style cross in Chapter 8 Funeral Designs).

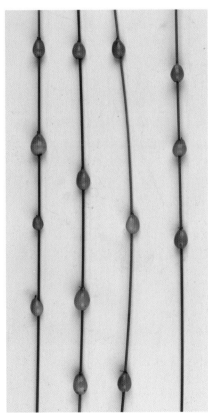

1. Thread coloured foam squares and Hypericum berries on to modelino-coloured cane.

2. Thread Hypericum berries onto Ficinea (flexi grass).

1. Turn the leaf face down and start to plait with the top fronds.

2. Fold the right-hand frond over into the middle.

3. Fold the left-hand frond over into the middle.

4. Continue plaiting...

5. Continue plaiting...

6. ...and once all the fronds are plaited in, secure with decorative wire.

Leaf Manipulation Techniques

By manipulating leaves and grasses using plaiting and rolling methods, distinctive features can be added to any floral design. Once you have mastered some of the ideas featured in this chapter, you might enjoy experimenting and creating some of your own design.

Palm plaiting

Use large palms – smaller varieties do not have the volume to create this pretty effect.

1. Turn the leaf face down on to a flat surface, for support and start to create a plait – using three fronds, take the right-hand outside frond fold over the middle, and then the left-hand outside

frond fold.

2. Fold the right-hand frond over into the middle.

3. Fold the left-hand frond over into the middle, and anchor it by folding the outside frond into the middle.

4&5. Continue this process, ensuring that

7. The finished leaf.

you keep maximum tension on the frond as you fold over, otherwise it will unravel.

6. Once you have used all the fronds, secure the ends by binding them

together – the design in the photograph has a decorative wire finish.

7. The finished article. (For details of this effect, see Limited tied design.)

Broad Leaf Manipulation

Leaves such as Aspidistra and Cordyline are ideal for folding, rolling and securing because they will not turn brown or bruise.

1. Split the Aspidistra leaf down the centre, then fold down the tips and secure them with a decorative wire finish. Spray with leaf shine (optional).

2. Cordyline leaf, folded and secured with a stapler: this fast method is commercially quicker if creating many folded leaves for multiple designs.

1. Split the leaf and fold it over, securing it with decorative wire.

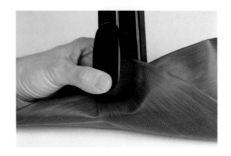

2. Fold the leaf and staple it.

Chapter 5
Arrangement Designs

Designing arrangements using the appropriate choice of floral foam offers the florist many varied creative design opportunities. Both modern and traditional styles can be produced, covering a massive selection of customer requirements. Whether it is for a gift or function or for corporate use, creating arrangements can be very satisfying, and also very commercial – with only trained florists having the skill required for creating such designs.

Floristry Foam

There are three different types of floristry foam that are extensively used in arrangement work: wet, coloured and dry foam.

Wet Foam

Wet foam is used to support stems that require water throughout the duration of their design life. This foam requires soaking in water prepared with flower food (although some brands have flower food impregnated into the foam itself). Foam must not be forcibly submersed into water, as this will result in irregular soaking, with some parts of the foam remaining dry – therefore the stems within these sections · will not be able to draw up water.
Place a foam brick into a bucket of room temperature water and allow it to soak and

submerge in its own time; once it has fully submerged, remove it from the water and allow it to drain. It is now ready for immediate use. Do not allow foam to dry out because re-soaking is not an option since irregular absorption will occur, and again, some stems will be left without water.

Coloured Foam

Coloured foam is mainly used for stems that require water, although it can be cut into ornate shapes and used as a decorate feature, for example star slices. This foam takes longer to soak fully than traditional foam. Repeat the soaking procedure as for wet foam. Again this medium is not suitable for re-soaking if it is allowed to dry out – ideally use it in a container where it is totally under water. It can dry out rapidly so frequent topping up is advised.

Dry Foam

This type of foam medium is not suitable for soaking and is only to be used for arrangements of silk or dry materials. It is denser than the other two types and is used to support the heavier stems of silk flowers and foliages. Be especially careful that you do not get dry foam dust in your eyes as it is an irritant and hard to remove; if you do, use an eye bath or seek urgent medical advice. Always wash your hands after use.

Using Foam

Once soaked (apart from dry foam), cut the foam to fit snugly in the chosen container – do not force it to fit, as this will squash the foam and compress the structure, making it difficult to insert stems. When inserting stems into the foam, ensure that you distribute them evenly across the width of the foam – this helps to create actual balance through a fair distribution of weight. Do not insert the stems too deeply – although they must be deep enough to be able to drink the water; if given a little tug they should not lift out.
Store all types of foam away from direct sunlight and damp conditions. All boxes of foam should be stored below eye level to avoid dust falling into the eyes.

Containers

All arrangements will require a container: after the design is completed some will be completely covered by foliage, but others will still be visible, so the container should always complement the style of the design and the choice of flowers. There are so many different types of container to choose from, it is worth considering their advantages and disadvantages – see table.

LEFT: Parallel arrangement.

Assorted ceramic containers.

The Packaging and Transport of Designs

All designs created for gift purposes benefit in appearance when gift wrapped with cellophane. Not only does this improve the presentation, it also protects the design from adverse weather during transit, and makes it easier to transport: remember PPT – presentation, protection, transportation (*see* Chapter 4 Tied Designs).

To gift wrap a design in a container, place the finished design onto a covered piece of card which is slightly wider than the design.

METHOD
1. Wrap one long piece of cellophane under the card, making sure that it is long enough to cover both sides of the design.

2. If you decide to fold the sides of the cellophane under on each side, therefore completely sealing up your design, be sure to cut air vents into the

Assorted metal containers.

Assorted basket containers.

Assorted plastic containers.

1. Cut the cellophane so that it is long enough to cover both sides of the design...

gift wrap to prevent it 'steaming up'.

3. Finish with a bow of your choice.

It is important that advice regarding transportation is given to the customer, so

2. ...and staple the sides together.

3. The finished gift wrap.

DIFFERENT CONTAINER TYPES		
Container type	Advantages	Disadvantages
Basket	Natural-looking Large variety of shapes and sizes Range of prices Easy to transport Lends itself to a large variety of designs from gift, wedding and sympathy Natural: wicker is bio-degradable	Can look old-fashioned Needs to be lined If placed outside can rot and attract woodlice
Ceramic	Large range of sizes and colours Heavy in weight keeps design stable Range of prices Both traditional and modern styles available	Can be expensive Heavy, which can make transportation of the design harder Larger containers can be expensive Can break
Plastic	Large range of colours, sizes and shapes available Cheap in price Does not need lining	Can look cheap and nasty Non bio-degradable Light in weight – designs could be unstable
Metal	Variety of shapes Modern style Range of prices Some metals are heavy in weight, which keeps the design stable	Can rust Needs lining if unpainted Can transfer temperature if placed in sunlight Can absorb the heat Can be expensive Certain metals are heavy, making transportation difficult
Glass	Large range of styles and shapes Recycled glass range available Broken glass could be recycled Selection of prices	Foam needs disguising with leaf material (unless coloured foam is used as a feature) High quality glassware can be expensive Can shatter and smash

that their design arrives home in one piece. This includes instructions to keep the design upright and to ensure that it is secure, and to avoid keeping it for any prolonged time in a vehicle – if conditions are too hot the flower material will wilt, too cold and it will perish.

Larger designs such as pedestal or reception arrangements may have to be constructed on site – if you do not have access to a van for transport. The other option is to partially construct the design in your workshop and then finish it on site.

....

Line Arrangement

MATERIALS
Fresh flowers and foliages
Five Gerberas (focal flowers)
Ten Pennisetum 'Black Magic' (filler flowers)
Ten Ruscus hypophyllum
Three Solidago (filler flowers)
One Arachniodes adiantiformis

Sundries
Container
Wet foam
Cellophane
Florist's knife and scissors

Suitability

As the name suggests, this arrangement consists of a staggered line of flowers, so it is essential to choose bold focal flowers. It is a front-facing design, and can be traditional or contemporary in appearance, depending on the flowers selected. It could be used in the following ways: in a restricted area such as on a windowsill or a hotel reception desk; a raised version would look well on a buffet table; or as a small gift arrangement, which could be suitable for someone young or old, male or female.

Storage (florist)

Store in a dark, cool area until delivery or collection, top up the foam with water as required, and mist if the plant materials used are suitable.

Care (customer)

Avoid placing the arrangement in direct sunlight or in a draught, near fruit, or where it would be vulnerable to fluctuating temperatures – for example in a car for prolonged periods. Top up the foam every few days with tepid water.

METHOD
1. Line the container with cellophane to ensure that the water doesn't leak out. First soak the foam, then cut it to fit the container – the foam must stand slightly proud of the container to allow the foliage to be placed in it at an angle, which enhances the finished profile of the design – and lightly chamfer the top edges of the foam.

2. Prepare all the cut material for use in foam by defoliating the lower part of the stems so that they enter the foam cleanly – if the lower leaves are left on and inserted into the foam the hole made will be overlarge and the stems may become unstable and fall out.

3. Proportion and scale are very important in this type of design. To determine how tall to make the foliage backbone, lay out the chosen focal flowers on a flat surface, spacing them out: an odd number of focal flowers is required, and the number can be increased or decreased according to the required size of the design and/or the size of the individual flower heads; then cut the foliage that will form the first back placement to fit four of the five flowers. This foliage backbone will comprise two-thirds of the overall design. Place this first piece to the back of the foam with a slight lean backwards – though

not too much, as the design may be placed against a wall or ledge.

4. Next cut the stem of the lower placement so that it is half of the backbone height: this becomes one third of the design and helps to create the correct proportion. Insert this stem into the front of the foam, angling the stem downwards.

5. Insert the foliage working from the back of the design to the front, so the pieces are progressively lower in height as you get to the front of the foam – the foliage will then appear to fan out from the middle of the foam to front and back. Be aware of keeping the profile correct, which is a slightly concave shape around the centre of the design.

6. Start to place the Gerbera (the focal flowers): imagine a centre axis down the centre of design, and insert the top and bottom focal flowers along this line.

7. Stagger the remaining Gerbera on either side of this axis, ensuring that the spacing is visually equal.

8. Place the flowers from the back of the design to the front so they reduce in height as you go.

9. Add the filler flowers down the focal flower line, creating a feeling of recession and aiming for maximum contrast. The fillers in the photograph are Pennisetum and Solidago. Ensure that the sides of the design are adequately covered with foliage, and that the back is concealed.

10. Complete your quality checks: ensure that all the materials are secure and free of damage, and that there is no foam showing, and finally mist the design.

1. Line the container with cellophane.

2 & 3. Measure the foliage backbone using four of the focal flowers as a guide.

4 & 5. Insert the foliage so that the tallest stems are at the back, creating a concave profile.

6. Insert the focal flowers at the top and bottom along an imaginary vertical axis.

7. Stagger the remaining focal flower on either side of the vertical axis.

8. Side view of the arrangement.

9. Add the filler foliages and flowers.

Seasonal Focal Flower Alternatives

Spring choice: Iris hollandica – modern
interpretation
Summer choice: Helianthus
Autumn choice: Dahlia
Winter choice: Brassica
Modern selection: Anthurium andreanum

Modern line arrangement using a choice of spring flowers.

Symmetrical Design

MATERIALS

Fresh flowers and foliages
Six Dianthus (focal flowers)
Three Eustoma (secondary flowers)
Nine Vernonica (secondary flowers)
Seven Origanum (oregano) (filler flowers)
Ten Ruscus hypophyllum
Five Arachniodes adiantiformis
Ten Equisetum stems

Sundries
Cylinder vase
Wet foam, cut to size
Dish
Frog – floral fix
Florist's knife and scissors

Suitability

This is a front-facing design with a symmetrical appearance. It can be made in a variety of sizes, so is very versatile: it is suitable as a gift, it could be used on a buffet table, or in a larger scale for a church pedestal or for function work. Although it is very traditional in shape, the flowers and foliages selected could give it a modern twist – for example bold colours and shapes, or using tropical flowers. As a gift it could suit most age groups and either gender (depending on the type and colour of the flowers and foliage chosen).

Storage (florist)

Store in a dark, cool area until delivery or collection, top up the foam with water as required, and mist if the plant materials used are suitable.

Care (customer)

Avoid placing the arrangement in direct sunlight or in a draught, near fruit, or where it would be vulnerable to fluctuating temperatures – for example in a car for prolonged periods. Top up the foam every few days with tepid water.

METHOD

1. One option for this design is to line the cylinder with Equisetum stems. Use a rubber band to hold the grass in place, and once it is all the way round, fix it firmly by tying a ribbon round it.

2. Soak the foam, then fix it to the tray using floral fix and frog.

3. Prepare all the cut material for use in the foam by defoliating the lower part of the stems so that they enter the foam cleanly – if the lower leaves are left on, this can make an overlarge hole in the foam so that ultimately the stems become unstable and fall out.

4. Proportion and scale are very important in this type of design. Working on the design principle of thirds, the tallest backbone foliage should be two thirds of the design (see Line Arrangement to judge this dimension), while the lower line placement should be one third of the backbone (this is achieved by measuring a piece of foliage that is half of the backbone piece). Each side measures two thirds of the backbone, so the three longest pieces should look in ascending order.

5. Insert the outer placements into the foam, with the tallest piece towards the back of the foam; do not let this piece lean back too much as the design then cannot be placed against a wall. The smallest outer placement should be at the front of the foam, together with the placements on either side, ensuring that a symmetrical outline is achieved.

6. Insert the foliage Ruscus hypophyllum from the back of the design to the front, so the pieces are progressively lower in height as you get to the front of the foam – the foliage will then appear to fan out from the middle of the foam to front and back.

7. Choose a different foliage – in this arrangement Arachniodes adiantiformis

1. Line the cylinder with Equisetum stems.

2. Add the dish and the foam to the vase.

3 & 4. Cut the foliage so the pieces selected are in ascending proportion.

5 & 6. Next, insert foliage from the back to the front of the design, creating a concave profile.

7. Add the side placements of foliage.

8. Add the top, bottom and focal Dianthus along an imaginary centre axis...

9. ...and then the remainder of the Dianthus staggered on either side of this axis.

10. Add Eustoma and Veronica diagonally across the design.

– for maximum contrast, inserting it on each side and being careful to keep the shape of the profile as a slight concave around the centre of the design.

8. Start to place the Dianthus (the focal flowers): imagine a central axis down the middle of the design, and insert the

top, bottom and focal flower down this line.

9. Stagger the remaining flowers on either side of this axis. Ensure the spacing is visually equal. Place the flowers from the back of the design to the front, as you work from top to bottom (see Line

Arrangement for guidance photo).

10. Place the Eustoma (secondary flower) in a staggered diagonal line across the width of the design, then place the Veronica (the other secondary flower) in a staggered diagonal line in the opposite direction.

11. Add the filler flowers.

11. Add Origanum (filler flowers) down the focal flower line, creating a feeling of recession and of maximum contrast.

12. Complete your quality checks: ensure that all the materials are secure and free of damage, and that they cover all the foam; if appropriate, mist the design.

Alternative Floral Choices

A traditional interpretation of this style of design requires the following floral choices: focal flowers that are bold in form, such as Rosa; filler flowers that are relatively small, such as Solidago; secondary flowers that are transitional in form such as Eustoma, and a couple of contrasting textures of foliage, such as Arachniodes and Eucalyptus.

Asymmetrical Design

MATERIALS
Fresh flowers and foliages
Four Eucalyptus 'Parvifolia'
Four Arachniodes adiantiformis
Nine Rosa 'Passion' (focal flowers)
Ten Alchemilla mollis (filler flowers)
Five Antirrhinum (secondary flowers)
Eight Cornus

Sundries
Container
Wet foam
Cellophane
Florist's knife and scissors

Suitability

This is a front-facing design where the sides of the design are different lengths but it still retains a visual balance (it is 'L'-shaped). The design might be sold in pairs, one being a mirror image of the other: like this they might be placed one on each end of a mantelpiece; alternatively they might be suitable for a buffet table, a church windowsill or a hotel reception desk. The design would be equally suitable as a gift or for a function, and it can be made to any dimension.

Storage (florist)

Store in a dark, cool area until delivery or collection, top up the foam with water as required, and mist if the plant materials used are suitable.

Care (customer)

Avoid placing the arrangement in direct sunlight or in a draught, near fruit, or where it would be vulnerable to fluctuating temperatures – for example in a car for prolonged periods. Top up the foam every few days with tepid water.

METHOD
1. Line the container with cellophane to ensure that it doesn't leak. Soak the foam and cut it to fit the container – the

foam must stand slightly proud of the container; then lightly chamfer the top edges of the foam.

2. Prepare all the cut material for use in foam, as before.

3. Proportion and scale are very important in this type of design. Working on the design principle of thirds, the tallest backbone foliage is two thirds of the design (see Line Arrangement above to find out how to judge this dimension), while the lower line placement is one third of the backbone – this piece of foliage should be half of the backbone piece so is the shorter side of the design. The longer, asymmetric side is two thirds of the backbone, so the three longest pieces should look as if they are in ascending order.

4. Insert the outer placements into the foam: place the tallest piece (Eucalyptus parvifolia) towards the back of the foam (do not let it lean back too far as the design then cannot be placed against a wall); the smallest (Eucalyptus – one third of the backbone) at the front of foam; and then the side pieces: Arachniodes adiantiformis one third of the backbone in length on one side, and Arachniodes adiantiformis two

thirds of the backbone in length on the other. It is a personal/customer choice as to whether the longest placement is to the right or the left, depending on whether a right- or a left-sided asymmetric look is wanted.

5. Insert the foliage Eucalyptus parvifolia from the back of the design to the front, so the pieces are progressively lower in height as you get to the front of the foam – the foliage will then appear to fan out from the middle of the foam. Choose a different foliage – here, Arachniodes adiantiformis is used – for maximum contrast, and insert on both sides.

6. Be careful to keep the shape of the profile: a slight concave around the centre of the design.

7. Start to place the Rosa (the focal flowers): imagine a centre axis down the middle of the design, and insert the top, bottom and focal flowers down this line. Stagger the remaining flowers on either side of this axis, making sure the spacing looks equal. Position the flowers from the back of the design to the front as you work your way down the vertical line of the arrangement.

8. Using the Antirrhinum (secondary flowers), create a staggered line going across the width of the design.

9. One option at this stage is to create a cornus caging, to emphasize the asymmetrical property of the design (see Wiring techniques in Chapter 6, for guidance).

10. Add Alchemilla mollis (filler flowers) down the focal flower line, creating a feeling of recession and making for maximum contrast.

2 & 3. Cut the foliage to the correct proportions.

4. Add the outer placements.

1. Cut the foam and chamfer the sides.

11. Complete your quality checks: ensure that all materials are secure and free of damage, and that all the foam is covered; and finally mist the design if it is appropriate to do so.

ALTERNATIVE IDEAS
See Symmetrical design (above) for ideas on alternative floral choices.

5. The front of the design.

6. The side profile.

7. Add the focal line of Rosa.

8. Add the diagonal line of Antirrhinum.

9. Add the cage of Cornus to emphasize the asymmetrical outline.

10. Add the filler flowers throughout.

Candle Arrangement Design

MATERIALS

Fresh flowers and foliages
Four Arachniodes adiantiformis
Two Eucalyptus 'Parvifolia'
One Ruscus racemosa
One Rosemary
Six Cymbidium orchid heads (focal flowers)
Eight Rosa 'Ranukula' (secondary flowers)

Sundries
One third of a block of wet foam
Tray
Floral fix
Strips of flat cane
Container
Chapel candle 165/50
Wires and pot tape
Florist's knife and scissors

Suitability

This design is suitable for a table arrangement for a dinner party, a wedding, or for anniversary celebrations; it would look particularly good on a round table or placed on a low coffee table. Note: Before taking an order for a venue, check that their fire regulations will accept candle designs.

Storage (florist)

Store in a dark, cool area until delivery or collection, top up the foam with water as necessary, and mist if appropriate to the materials used. Attach a candle care card to the design.

Care (customer)

Avoid placing the design in direct sunlight or in a draught, near fruit, or where it would be vulnerable to fluctuating temperatures. Top up the foam with tepid water every few days. Be aware of the health and safety issues of using a lit candle; never leave the design unattended when the candle is lit. Be especially careful when young children and/or pets are present.

METHOD

1. Soak the foam, then anchor it in the tray using pot tape, ensuring that the two pieces of pot tape are wide enough apart to accommodate the candle. Prepare the candle to secure into the foam. Using pot tape, stick four cocktail sticks about the base of the candle (alternatively use candle cups or 'hair pin' 90g wires).

2. Attach the tray to the top of the container using floral fix, making sure that the tray is secure. Then place the candle in the desired position – it is essential that it is very secure and straight.

3. Prepare all the cut material for use in foam by defoliating the lower part of the stems so that they enter the foam cleanly – if the lower leaves are left on, the hole

1. Assembling the hardware for the arrangement.

2. Fix the tray with the foam and the candle onto the cylinder.

3 & 4. Angle the Arachniodes, first a line to conceal the cylinder top, and then round the base of the candle.

made will be overlarge and the stems will become loose and unstable and will fall out.

4. Insert the Arachniodes adiantiforms: first place a line round the rim of the container, ensuring that the foliage pieces conceal the 'join' between the container rim and the tray attachment. Then add smaller pieces round the base of the candle, making sure that none could interfere with the candle when it is lit.

5. Add the remainder of the smaller foliage pieces until the foam is well covered and a pleasing profile has been achieved.

6. Insert the individual orchid heads (the focal flowers) at regular intervals round the candle.

7. Add the Rosa on either side of the orchids, both top and bottom.

8. Swirls of flat cane could also be inserted throughout the design as an additional option.

9. Finally check that all the materials are secure and free of damage, and that all the foam is covered; in particular ensure that nothing potentially flammable is too near the candle. Mist the design if appropriate to the materials used.

Note: Always add a candle care card to the design, to ensure that the customer is aware of the health and safety risks of a lit candle.

5. Add the remainder of the foliage pieces.

6. Add the focal flowers, in this arrangement the Cymbidium orchids.

7. Add the secondary flowers, the Rosa.

8. Cane swirls could also be added to the design.

Basket Design

MATERIALS
Fresh flowers and foliages
Three Eucalyptus 'Parvifolia'
Four Pittosporum tobira
Ten Veronica (secondary flowers)
Six Eustoma russellianum (secondary flowers)
Nine Rosa 'Heaven' (focal flowers)
Five Pepper (filler flowers)

Sundries
Basket
Wet foam
Cellophane
Florist's knife and scissors

Suitability

Baskets are available in many sizes and colours – some have handles some do not, they are universally popular with most age groups. Basket designs therefore can be suitable for a wide range of occasions: bridesmaids, gifts, anniversaries, birthdays, mother's day, birth of baby girl and even sympathy designs.

Storage (florist)

Store in a dark, cool area until delivery or collection, top up the foam with water as required, and mist if the plant materials used are suitable.

Care (customer)

Avoid placing the arrangement in direct sunlight or in a draught, near fruit, or where it would be vulnerable to fluctuating temperatures – for example in a car for prolonged periods. Top up the foam with tepid water every few days. Place a mat under the design to protect polished surfaces.

METHOD

1. Soak the floral foam, and line the basket with cellophane (even if it is pre-lined, to prevent any potential leakage of water). Cut the foam to fit, lightly chamfering the top edges. Allow the foam to stand proud of the basket rim.

2. Prepare all the cut material for use in foam by defoliating the lower part of the stems so that they enter the foam cleanly – as before.

3. Add a line of foliage, in this case Eucalyptus, so that it extends slightly over the edge of the basket, but being careful that the pieces are not too high, which would spoil the line of the handle and make it difficult to carry the basket when the design is complete.

4. Add a second line of a different foliage, in this case Pittosporum, across the centre of the design from left to right; angle the outer positions downwards to conceal the foam and cellophane packing.

5. Add a line of roses (the focal flowers) from left to right across the middle of the basket; in this particular arrangement three roses have been grouped together in the centre to create a central focal area – alternatively one larger focal flower could be used.

1. Line the basket with cellophane and add soaked foam.

3. Add a line of Eucalyptus foliage.

4. Add a line of Pittosporum tobira foliage from left to right across the basket.

5. Insert a line of Rosa.

6. Insert a diagonal line of Veronica.

7. Insert a diagonal line of Eustoma, and fill in with Pepper.

6. Next place a line of secondary flowers diagonally across the design – here, Veronica have been used.

7. Place another diagonal line of a different secondary flower – Eustoma has been used in this design. Add some smaller filler flowers – here, Pepper has been used – recessed across the centre from left to right, to add visual interest to this design.

8. Ensure that all the materials are secure and free from damage, and that all the foam is covered. Mist the design if the plant material used is suitable. Add a gift card with care card details.

Alternative Arrangements

There are many different styles of basket on the market, ranging from traditional to contemporary, and the flowers chosen for an arrangement should be appropriate to the basket style selected.

....

Container without a Handle

MATERIALS
Fresh flowers and foliages
Six Germinis (focal flower)
Five small Rosa
Six Tulipa 'Purple Rain'
One Solidaster (filler)
Eight Freesia
Five Ruscus hypophllyum
Four Eucalyptus 'Baby Blue'
Seven Arachniodes adiantiformis

Sundries
One container
Two blocks of wet foam
Cellophane
Florist's knife and scissors

Suitability

This design can be viewed all the way round, so it can be positioned in the centre of a table – for example for a wedding or a function – or on a low coffee table. But whether as a gift or for function work, this is a versatile design that can be contemporary or traditional in character depending on the choice of container and flowers.

Storage (florist)

Store in a dark, cool area until delivery or collection, top up the foam with water as required, and mist if the plant materials used are suitable.

Care (customer)

Avoid placing the arrangement in direct sunlight or in a draught, near fruit, or where it would be vulnerable to fluctuating temperatures – for example in a car for prolonged periods. Top up the foam every few days with tepid water.

METHOD
1. Line the container with cellophane to ensure that no water leaks out. Soak the foam, then cut it to fit the container so that it stands slightly proud of it; lightly chamfer the top edges of the foam.

2. Prepare all the cut material for use in foam, as before.

3. Insert the Arachniodes foliage around the bottom edge, angling it downwards to conceal the foam, and keeping these side pieces the same size so as to enhance the outline shape of the container. Then insert the remainder of the Arachniodes across the foam.

1 & 2. Line the container with cellophane and insert the soaked foam.

3. Add the Arachniodes foliage, covering the rim of the container.

4. Add the Ruscus throughout the design.

5. Place one Germini in the centre, and the remainder around it in a circle.

6. Add the Rosa, slightly recessed, in between the Germini.

7. Add the remainder of the flowers.

4. Insert a contrasting foliage – in this case Ruscus – throughout the design.

5. Place a Germini (focal flower) in the centre of the design, and then position the others equally spaced in a circle around it.

6. Place the Rosa in between the Germinis, cutting the stems shorter to help give a sense of recession.

7. Add the Freesia, Tulipa and solidaster as shown in the photograph.

8. To give this design special distinction, add bundles of coloured sticks, as shown (see Additional wiring techniques in Chapter 6 Weddings, for guidance).

8. Give the design special distinction by adding bundles of coloured sticks.

9. Finally, check that all the materials are secure and undamaged, and that all the foam is covered. Add a gift card with care card details. Mist the design if the materials are appropriate to do so.

Coloured Foam Design

MATERIALS
Fresh flowers and foliages
Three Fatsia japonica
Four Liatris
One Hypericum 'Envy Flair'
Six Rosa 'Marie Claire'
Two Trachelium 'Lake Superior'

Sundries
One container
Two blocks of lime-coloured foam
Cubes of lime-coloured foam
Five dyed green willow
Four green modelino cane
Florist's knife and scissors
Leafshine

Suitability

Coloured foam helps to create a wide range of modern designs, which could be used for various purposes: as a gift for either a man or a woman; for corporate design; in a hotel reception area or a wine bar; in a beauty salon or a hairdresser's; or as a placement on a registrar's table for a modern wedding.

Storage (florist)

Store in a dark, cool area until delivery or collection; top up the foam regularly with water; and mist according to the materials used. Inform the customer that this sort of design must be topped up with tepid water every day, as coloured foam needs additional hydration care.

DIFFERENCES BETWEEN MODERN AND TRADITIONAL DESIGNS

Modern	Traditional
More than one visual focal area	One focal area
Stems are often vertically placed only	Stems radiate from a central focal point
Stripped stems are part of the design	Stems are concealed within the design
Large-headed materials can form the external edges of the design	Transitional use of materials (the smaller material is used at the edges)
Even numbers of focal materials can be used	Odd numbers of materials are used, especially with focal floral selection
Greater significance of the elements: texture, form, space, colour and line	All elements are subtly used
Frequent selection of linear bold materials for placements	Variety of all forms, and not always an all-bold choice
Mostly the outline shape is rectangular	The outline shape is generally triangular
Containers are geometric – square or rectangular	Most containers, including tapered ones, can be used.
Blocking and grouping create the base of the design	Recession is created by the use of colour or shorter placements
Materials are grouped together, either vertically or horizontally	Materials are staggered along the focal line

Care (customer)

Avoid placing the design in direct sunlight, in a draught, near fruit, or where it would be vulnerable to fluctuating temperatures. Top up the foam with tepid water every day.

METHOD

1. Soak and cut the coloured foam to fit your chosen container – be very careful not to make any mistakes with cutting or placing the materials into the foam, as you will not be concealing them as with traditional foam.

2. Cut three pieces of green willow and place them off centre on one side of the container; next cut two pieces of green willow two thirds of the length of the first, and place them on the other side.

3. Prepare all the cut material for use in foam by defoliating the lower part of the stems – as before.

4. Cut four Liatris and place them firmly into the foam as shown, with three stems staggered on one side within the willow and one on the other.

1. Carefully cut the coloured foam to fit the container.

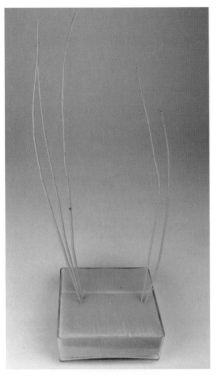

2. Add the coloured willow.

4. Insert the Liatris.

5. Cut the Fatsia leaves, first giving them a spray with leafshine (follow the manufacturer's instructions on ventilation); insert two leaves at the base of the dominant side creating a layered feel, and one on the other.

6. Next cut the Rosa, and place them in staggered order, with four stems one side and two on the other. Then cut the Trachelium very short and insert them low to the foam so as to conceal the area at the base of the placements and add visual recession.

7. An optional decorative detail is to remove the berries of the Hypericum and thread them onto the modelino cane, interspersing a cube of coloured foam between each berry. Then put the cane into the foam, and weave and twist it around creating an interesting shape; secure the end of cane on to a fixing point with decorative wire (see Additional wiring techniques in Chapter 6 Weddings, for guidance).

8. Check that all the materials are secure, and top up the foam with water. Gift wrap if appropriate, and add a care card.

Coloured foam opens up a whole new set of design options, from the choice of container to the best show foam, which needs to be carefully selected, along with suitable fresh materials. Such a modern style works best with bold, modern flowers.

ALTERNATIVE IDEAS
By using pink foam and pink Rosa instead of orange, the design would then be suitable for the birth or christening of a baby girl. An option for a boy would be to use cream-coloured foam with blue larkspur instead of Liatris, and white Rosa with a blue-headed pin.

5. Insert the layered Fatsia leaves.

6. Add the focal Rosa, in staggered positions.

7. Add distinction by using threaded cane.

Parallel Design

MATERIALS
Fresh flowers and foliages
Four Rosa 'Blizzard'
Four Trachelium 'Dafne'
Three Allium 'Purple Sensation'
Two Equisetum
Twelve Galax leaves
Three Ornithogalum thyrsoides
Amount of Reindeer moss
One Pittosporum tenufolium

Sundries
Half a block of wet foam
Container
Florist's knife and scissors

Suitability

This is a very modern design, suitable as a gift for man or woman, for a corporate setting, for a windowsill in a modern place of worship, or for any area where a long, thin design is required. Stems are placed parallel to each other or side by side, and with exactly the same distance between them: therefore the lines never meet or radiate from the same point. Visual and actual texture is very important in this style of design, and flower choice should be linear and bold for the vertical placements and textured for the low placements.

Storage (florist)

Store in a dark, cool area until delivery or collection, top up the foam with water as required, and mist if the plant materials used are suitable.

Care (customer)

Avoid placing the arrangement in direct sunlight or in a draught, near fruit, or where it would be vulnerable to fluctuating temperatures – for example in a car for prolonged periods. Top up the foam every few days with tepid water.

METHOD

1. Cut the foam to fit the container, and soak.

2. Prepare all the cut materials for use in foam by defoliating the lower part of the stems – as before.

3. Group flowers of the same sort together,

and insert the stems into the foam so that they are all parallel to each other; ensure that the stems can be seen, and that there is negative space between the stems.

4. Use materials that create the maximum contrast of form and texture to cover the base of the foam – cut them short and insert them firmly. Put contrasting textures next to each other – for example, fluffy Trachelium next to smooth-cupped Galax leaves (see the wiring techniques section in Chapter 6 for guidance).

Alternative Flower Choice

For the tall linear plant material choose Liatris iris, Dianthus, Helianthus, Aconitum, Antirrhinum, Craspedia, Eremurus, Gladiolus, Cornus.
For plants of low textural interest use Tillandsia (Spanish moss), large Hedera helix (ivy), Asparagus umbellatus, Limonium, Brunia.

For the container, a geometric shape – a rectangle or square – works best with this design.

1. Cut and insert the foam into the container.

3. Place the taller flowers of the same sort in groups together.

4. Cover the foam with textured materials.

Chapter 6
Wedding Designs

During a consultation with a bride, many considerations must be taken into account whilst deciding on appropriate floral designs.

A florist must have a wide knowledge of the availability of seasonal flowers so as to be able to recommend appropriate flower choices. Never promise a particular flower because it will be subject to availability at auction, so inform the bride that you reserve the right to substitute her first choice with the best alternative flower/foliage. Also fashion changes, and a florist needs to keep up to date with current trends and techniques; therefore keep a portfolio of past designs and wedding reference books, or laptop presentations, to help with bridal consultations.

Once the consultation has taken place, write a quotation and take a deposit to secure the booking. You may require the customer to sign and return a copy of the quotation to say that they agree to its contents. If hiring any vases, mirrored plates and suchlike, do create a separate hire agreement taking both a payment for hire and a deposit in the event of breakages or non-return of hired items. About a month before the wedding date take a further 50 per cent of the payment, and with two weeks to go, ask for the balance. To be paid on the day of the wedding is a risky business: what if either the bride or the groom fails to turn up? Who will pay for the flowers?

LEFT: Bridal bouquet in a foam holder.

THE WEDDING ORDER	
Questions	Factors to be considered
Height of the bride	Size of the bouquet
Style of the bride's gown, including fabric texture, colour, finish (pearls or crystals)	Style of the bouquet: down shower, posy, over the arm
Theme of the wedding: colour, seasonal, historical, other	Flower choice
Date of the wedding (if the wedding date falls in a peak time the flowers will be expensive so you will need to take this into account when quoting prices for designs)	The availability of particular flowers – for the best price, pick flowers that are in season and therefore readily available
Bridesmaids – how many and their ages	Mature bridesmaids need different designs to that of younger maids
Hair colouring and hair style	For headwear designs
The wedding party	Button holes, corsages etc.
Thank-you gifts	Are floral thank-you gifts required, as hand-tied flowers or plants
Budget	Budget, which will influence flower choice and how many designs are made
Venue décor	The type of designs – for the top table, buffet designs, garlanding (these should match the age and style of the buildings)
Ceremony décor	The type of designs required for pew ends, garlanding etc (again, match the age and style of the buildings)
Delivery of the designs	How many delivery addresses, as for example the bride's home, the reception hotel, the church

Wiring Techniques

Wiring is a skill that every florist must master – it sets the trade professional apart from the amateur. It takes practice to become neat and to use the appropriate technique and weight of wire for the relevant flower/foliage. Wiring is used for support and anchorage, for binding materials together, and for lengthening and strengthening the stem.

Support Wiring

This technique strengthens and lengthens the individual stems of both flowers and foliage. It is mainly used in wedding work, for wired bouquets, corsages and buttonholes. The weight of the wire selected is important: too heavy and it could shatter the stem of the flower, too light and it will not be strong enough to support the stem. A rough guide to know whether or not you have selected the correct wire weight is the 'bounce test': support wire the stem, then hold the wire between forefinger and thumb – if the wire stays horizontal but not too rigid it is fine; if it is too rigid change it for a lighter weight wire, but if the weight of the flower head bends the wire over, then a heavier wire is needed.

All visible wires should be covered with floral tape, and there are two main sorts on the market: Parafilm (registered trade mark), which has a plastic texture; or Stemtex (registered trade mark), with a papery texture. If using the latter, score round the reel with a knife, thus making it half the width, which is much neater for small wired work such as buttonholes. After support wiring your materials it is important to tape them quickly, as this slows the process of dehydration – though if support wiring for funeral work, eg. gerberas and roses, taping is not necessary.

INTERNAL WIRING

This technique is used on semi-hollow stems and some fleshy stems. The wire is inserted up through the middle of the stem until the resistance of the calyx (the base of the flower) is reached. By strengthening the stem in this way you can insert it more easily into the foam.

FLORISTRY WIRES AND THEIR USES	
Gauge	Uses
28mm (green)	Very fine wire – for support wiring lightweight flowers, cross stitching
32mm (green and silver)	Available as reel wire – for binding together wedding work. Available as separate lengths of wire – for support wiring lightweight flowers; also for stitching ivy leaves
38mm (green)	For support wiring small flowers and stitching leaves
46mm (green)	For support wiring medium flowers and stitching leaves
56mm (reel wire black uncoated) (green)	Reel wire – for heavyweight binding such as door wreaths. Separate individual wires for support wiring medium flowers such as roses, and pinning materials into/onto the medium
71mm (green)	For support wiring medium to large flowers, and pinning materials into/onto the medium
90mm (green)	Support wiring heavy materials, mainly foliages, and pinning materials into/onto the medium
120mm (uncoated black)	Very heavy wire – useful for making hooks on wreaths or support wires on a framework
Decorative wires	Available in a wide range of weights, colours and finishes – for decorative purposes, and for support wire in modern work where the wiring should be seen

PIPPING

This is a variation on internal wiring, where the wire is inserted through a short cut stem and out through the centre of the flower head – bend over the wire to form a hook, then pull the hook down into the flower head until it is out of sight. This is a great technique for small-headed flowers such as spray Dianthus or spray Rosa for wedding work.

wrapped around the stem – avoid twisting the wire too many times round the stem as this will make the flower bulky. Ideal flowers for this technique are Gerberas, Dianthus and roses.

Bend the wire ends down on each side of the main stem vein, effectively forming a loop, and twist them together at the base of the leaf.

Pipping.

External wiring.

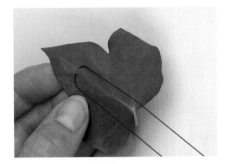

Stitch the wire through the back of the leaf.

SEMI-INTERNAL WIRING

With a fleshy stem such as Tulipa, instead of inserting a wire right up the centre of the whole stem, insert it into the stem about 5cm under the flower head, push it up through the middle of stem (this can be quite fiddly) from where you inserted it; twist the excess wire down around the outside of the stem.

EXTERNAL WIRING

The wire is inserted into the stem at the base of the flower, the calyx, and then

CROSS STITCHING

Cut off the stem and insert the wire up the centre of the remaining stem until it meets the resistant of the calyx. Then thread another lighter wire across the base of the flower, and bend the cross wire down until it lies on each side of the stem – this additional wire keeps the tension of the flower on the stem and the first wire. This is a good technique for preparing individual heads such as Cymbidium (see Wired Orchid Bouquet).

STITCHING

This technique is applied to foliages. Take a leaf and turn it over, so you are working on its reverse side: start a third of the way up the leaf by making a small stitch through the main vein.

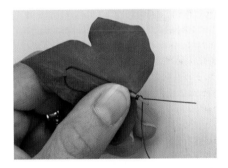

Secure the wire round the base of the leaf.

Semi-internal wiring. The wire is inserted into the stem about 5cm from the head, then wound externally down the stem.

Cross-stitch wiring.

The finished wiring.

Leave a short length of natural stem to wind the wires round: this then creates a strengthened 'stem'.

Green wire is best used for stitching; it is ideal for ivy leaves.

Mount Wiring

Mount wire is used to add length to the stems of plant material – these can then be inserted into foam or added into the binding point of wired work. If the stem is already support wired, the mount wire will need to be heavier – for example, mini Cymbidium support wired with 70mm wire needs a 90mm mount wire. The weight of the stem will dictate whether a single or double leg mount is required: lighter stems will need a single leg mount, heavier stems a double leg mount.

Single leg mount: Wrap the wire round the base of the stem so that only one wire is left exposed. This is suitable for smaller stems, such as Rosa.

Double leg mount: Wrap the wire round the base of the stem so that two wires are left exposed. This is suitable for heavy foliages.

Units

This term applies to an assembly of materials that are mounted together; the different units are known as branching, natural and ribbed.

Branching unit: The same materials are used, for example only Hedera leaves; several support-wired leaves are taped together and then arranged to resemble a branch, with the small leaves at top, increasing in size to the larger leaves at the bottom. Branching units enable you to extend stem lengths. It is a great technique for corsages.

Natural unit: This technique uses a couple

Single leg mount.

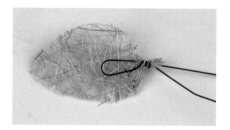

Double leg mount.

Branching unit.

Natural unit.

of stems of the same material mount wired together in either a single or a double leg mount. Using several stems together increases the visual impact. It is a useful technique for wedding work.

Ribbed unit: Materials are taped onto a stay wire for support; they may be all the same, or mixed – for example Hedera leaves and Hyacinthus. This is a good technique for Alice bands described later in this chapter.

Binding

Binding describes a particular technique of attaching and securing – for example, of attaching moss to a wreath ring, and securing together the wire stems of a corsage: no natural stems should ever be bound into a binding point – all natural stems should end at the binding point, and the mount wires begin here.

Additional Wiring Techniques

The following techniques are used for decorative and supportive methods.

Decorative Stitching: This technique follows the same requirements as stitching an ivy leaf, but using decorative wire so that the wire becomes part of the feature. (This technique is used in the project Wired Bridal Posy.)

Bundling: Again, decorative coloured wire is used. Wind the wire several times neatly round the centre of a couple of coloured sticks. This technique could also be used to create bundles of cinnamon sticks for use in winter designs. (This technique is used in the project Container without a Handle in Chapter 5 Arrangement Designs.)

Cross stitching: This technique is used to secure fruit to arrangements/ door wreaths: using two heavy wires, cross stitch

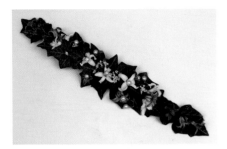

Ribbed unit.

Decorative stitching.

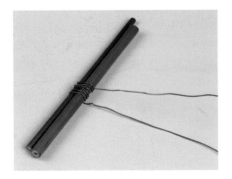

Bundling.

WIRED BRIDAL WORK – ADVANTAGES AND DISADVANTAGES	
Advantages	Disadvantages
A variety of outline shapes and designs can be made	The materials are not in water, which may affect freshness
The materials are all firmly secured	The techniques require a higher level of skill so the designs are more expensive
Light designs can be constructed, which are well balanced when held	Wiring techniques take time and are labour intensive
A more elegant handle can be made if the bouquet is wired	

for a more natural effect use raffia or paper-coloured wire. This creates an effective contemporary structure. (This technique is used in the project Tropical Hand tie in Chapter 4 Tied Designs, and in the projct Asymmetric Design in Chapter 5 Arrangements.)

Cupping: Using a Galax leaf – alternatively use an ivy leaf such as a large Hedera – twist the leaf round as shown then secure it by piercing the wire through the base of the leaf. Finish with a single leg wire mount. (This technique is used in the parallel design project in Chapter 5 Arrangement Designs.)

Cross stitching.

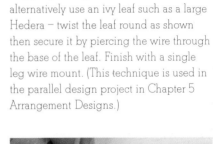

1. Twist the Galax leaf...

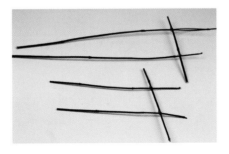

Simple caging.

2. ... then pierce the wire through the base of the leaf.

as photographed, then pull all four ends down and twist them together. (This technique is used in the project Loose Open Posy in Chapter 8 Funeral Designs.)

Simple caging: Using Cornus or coloured willow, cut and bind over the joins with matching or contrasting decorative wire;

Tied Bridal Designs

Bridal Single Flower Design

MATERIALS

Fresh flowers and foliages
Twenty Rosa 'Heaven' (focal flowers)
Four trails of Hedera helix

Sundries
Flat frame 20cm diameter
32-gauge reel wire
Green pot tape 16mm
Wired organza ribbon
Headed pins
Florist's knife and scissors
Wire cutters
Wet spray dispenser
Floral tape

SUITABILITY
This posy is suitable for the bride or an
adult bridesmaid.

Storage (florist)
Store in dark, cool area; leave the stems in
water, and mist if appropriate to the
materials used. Before delivery dry off the
stems and add the ribbon finish. There are
two methods of transporting the bouquet:
either in a covered box, where a hole is cut
in the top of the box and the finished
bouquet inserted into the hole so that it
sits flush with box – you may wish to soak
some cotton wool with water and place the
cut stems on top of them. Alternatively
insert the stems in a vase with minimum
water. Both methods will help to keep the
stems hydrated.

Care (customer)
Keep the bouquet away from direct heat;
handle with care.

METHOD
1. Tape three 120gsm wires with brown
   floral tape, and attach them to the inner
   part of the flat frame; fold them over and

1. Bend over and tape the wires and attach
them to the frame.

2. Pull the three support wires to the
centre and tape them together.

3. Attach the Hedera helix to the frame.

4. The completed frame.

6. Insert the Rosa into the frame, spiralling
the stems as you go.

7. Create a domed profile.

8. Tie off the bouquet and add two strips of pot tape.

9. Add the ribbon to embellish the handle.

10. Finish off the handle with headed pins.

tape them so they are secure with no sharp ends protruding.

2. Fold the three taped wires to the middle, and bend them at a 45-degree angle to form a handle; then tape them together, and trim the length of the handle to avoid having to cut through with secateurs later. With a larger frame use four wires to make the handle stronger.

3. Using the single leg method (see Wiring techniques), attach 32-gauge reel wire to the end of the ivy and to the frame; then wrap the ivy round the frame, securing the other end on the frame with wire.

4. Continue this method of attaching ivy on to the frame until it is completely covered.

5. Prepare all the cut materials as for the tied designs, by stripping all the lower foliage and the cut stems.

6. Hold the frame by the handle and thread the rose stems into the frame, starting at the centre and working round the frame, spiralling the stems (see Chapter 4 Tied Designs for guidance) as you go.

7. Continue to place the flowers into the frame until the middle is completely filled in. The bouquet should have a lovely domed profile, and for this it is

11. The finished bouquet.

important to choose your cultivar of rose carefully: you will need a round-shaped head with a flat profile to achieve the best look – some long-headed cultivars do not 'bond' very well together and may leave 'gaps'.

8. Tie the bouquet with string and secure it with pot tape, then twist the pot tape so that it is sticky side up; also bind pot tape further down the stem: this will help secure the ribbon handle when you attach it.

9. Stick the ribbon onto the pot tape, and bind it down the handle until you reach the second band of pot tape; then cut the ribbon.

10. Finish off the ribbon handle with decorative pins. Cut the flower stems neatly, about 20cm from the binding point: too long or too short and the bouquet will be difficult to hold.

11. Check that the copper frame is completely concealed with ivy; remove any damaged leaves or petals. Spray with water. Place the bouquet in a vase with a shallow water level (so as not to get the ribbon wet) until delivery time.

ALTERNATIVE FLOWER IDEAS
An alternative idea is to use roses of more than one colour. Or you could use the ivy frame but use mixed flowers and small foliages instead of just roses.

Natural Posy
MATERIALS
Fresh flowers and foliages
Six Eustoma
Five Rosa 'Aqua'
Eight Convallaria (lily of the valley flowers and leaves)
Two Eucalyptus 'Parvifolia'

Sundries
String
Scissors
6mm pot tape
Satin pink ribbon

SUITABILITY
This natural posy shape makes a bouquet that is suitable for the bride or her bridesmaids; for a civil wedding ceremony; as a presentation for a visiting VIP; or as a small gift for any occasion.

Storage (florist)
Store in a dark, cool area with the stems in shallow water; shortly before delivery or collection dry out the stems, and finish off by binding them with a satin ribbon. Deliver either in a lidded box – cut a hole in the lid and insert the finished bouquet so that it sits flush with the lid (you may wish to put some water-soaked cotton wool in the box and place the cut stems on it) – or insert the stems in a vase with a small

amount of water. Both methods will help keep the stems hydrated.

Care (customer)
Avoid leaving the bouquet in direct sunlight; handle with care.

METHOD
1. Prepare all the materials as for tied designs, by stripping all the lower foliage and cut stems.

2. Create a core of foliages with the Eustoma head at the centre, then add the remainder of the materials, spiralling the stems (see Chapter 4 Tied Designs for guidance on spiralling) as you work your way round. Add three of the Convallaria, again spiralling the stems, spacing them evenly round the core.

3. Add the five remaining Eustoma flower heads, creating a posy shape.

1. Prepare the cut materials.

2. Create a centre core of flowers and foliage.

3. Add a circle of Eustoma, spiralling the stems.

4. Add the Rosa, retaining the posy outline.

5. Add a collar of Convallaria leaves.

6. Create a binding point with pot tape.

7. Add the ribbon bow to the handle.

4. Add the five Rosa in between the Eustoma flower heads.

5. To finish, add the five remaining Convallaria equally with some additional eucalyptus and a collar of Convallaria leaves.

6. Using 6mm pot tape, create a binding point – once bound all the way round, twist the pot tape so that it is sticky side up: this will secure the ribbon bow.

7. Add the ribbon bow over the binding pot tape to finish.

8. Finally check for damaged materials, also check that all the materials are secure, and that the stems are clean of all foliages and trimmed neatly. Mist spray if appropriate to the materials.

ALTERNATIVE MATERIALS

This design works best with small-headed flowers and foliages, as these create a natural feel to the design: for flowers, use Chamelaucium, Convallaria, spray Dianthus, spray Rosa, spray Chrysanthemum, Gypsophila, Mimosa, anemones, Muscari, Skimma, Hypericum, Eustoma, Veronica, Lathyrus odoratus (sweet pea), Alchemilla Ranunculus. For foliage, use Pittosporum tenufolium, Rosmarinus (rosemary), Asparagus virgatus (tree fern).

The design can be created without a foliage collar, or use Arachniodes adiantiformis (leather leaf) or small Monstera leaves.

Bridal Designs in Holders

Loose Open Bridal Design
This design is created in a bridal belle holder.

MATERIALS
Fresh flowers and foliages
Nine Rosa 'Heaven' (focal flowers)
Five Nigella (filler flowers)
Three Eustoma russellianum (secondary flowers)
Three Myrtus communis (myrtle)

A selection of bridal holders.

Three Eucalyptus parvifolia
Three Galax leaves

Sundries
Bridal holder with wet foam
Decorative cord, double-sided tape
Decorative wires
Decorative headed pins
Florist's knife and scissors

SUITABILITY
This design is suitable for a bridesmaid's posy or for the bride herself; for a civil ceremony; or as a presentation bouquet. A nice touch is to cover the bridal holder with fabric/cord/ribbon/silk petals/fresh leaves/spray in colours that match and compliment the colours of the wedding.

Storage (florist)
Store this posy upright and in the dark; keep it cool, and mist spray if appropriate. Deliver in a lidded box: cut a hole in the lid and insert the finished posy so that it sits flush with the lid.

Care (customer)
Store the bouquet out of direct sunlight and heat until you are ready to use it.

METHOD
1. Stick double-sided tape down the handle; a further option is to put a large-headed pin into the base. Wind the cord on to the holder, starting at the base and working along the handle, keeping the tension on the cord. Next, dunk the frame into a bucket (being careful not to get the cord wet) for just five seconds – any longer and the foam could disintegrate and drip down the customer's dress.

2. To create the posy outline, work out the preferred diameter by cutting two

1. Stick the cord to the bridal holder.

2. Measure the foliage.

THE ADVANTAGES AND DISADVANTAGES OF BRIDAL HOLDERS	
Advantages	Disadvantages
The flowers are able to take up moisture	The design can be heavy to hold
Quick and easy to make	The plastic handle looks cheap
The handle can be decorated	The materials are not secured
Cheaper to make – a lower level of skills is required	Non-trained florists can 'have a go', not always with good results
A variety of sizes is available – some holders are 'faced'	Can drip, or the foam may crumble if over-soaked
Wet or dry foam can be used, and it is possible to glue materials into dry foam	Some larger or heavy-stemmed materials will not go into the foam
	The florist is limited as to the styles that can be made using foam

pieces of outline foliage, in this case eucalyptus – place them one on each side of the holder to judge the diameter.

3. Once this length has been determined, cut fifteen to twenty pieces of foliage the same length.

4. To create the faced design the posy outline needs to be angled – use the foam holder frame as a helpful guide. In the bottom segment angle the foliage downwards, and in the top back segment angle it upwards; the foliage in the side segments joins the outline from top and bottom, creating a diagonal line. (Alternatively buy a ready-faced foam holder.)

5. Fill the front of the design with foliage, using shorter pieces to create a slightly concave outline; mix in myrtle to help create a feeling of recession.

6. Next, add five Rosa to the outside edge, equally spaced – to help with this, add 90mm-gauge wires as markers, which enables you to adjust the spacing without making large holes in the foam. Keep the angle of the stems the same as the outer foliage. A useful tip is that if you misplace material in the foam, 'fill' the incorrect hole with a stem, thereby plugging the foam – otherwise the hole could become so large that it compromises the foam, and you may have to start again.

7. Add the focal centre Rosa – a useful tip is to hold out the bouquet at arm's length and insert the Rosa so that the centre eye looks straight at you. Think also of the profile: this centre Rosa is the focal point and so should stand slightly proud of the design.

8. Add the last three Rosa into the design, and the remaining flowers: the Eustoma (the secondary flowers), spacing them between the Rosa but slightly lower so as to continue the feeling of recession, and lastly the Nigella heads (filler flowers) – this colour choice also helps the feeling of recession.

9. As an extra option you could add some accessories, such as beads, decorative

3. Cut the other foliage pieces to the same length.

4. 'Face' the foliage as you insert the pieces into the holder.

5. Add the rest of the foliage.

6. Insert five Rosa on the outside edge, using wires as a guide.

7. Add the centre Rosa, creating a domed profile.

8. Add the Eustoma flowers, slightly lower so as to help the feeling of recession.

9. As an option, add decorative wired picks.

wire, pre-made wired picks, feathers. Finish the 'back' of the design by concealing the foam and the frame with single flat leaves – never place flowers at the back, as this could confuse a customer and might tempt them to hold the posy incorrectly.

10. Lastly, make your routine quality checks: first, hold the bouquet in front of a mirror to check the flowers for equal spacing; check also for damaged petals, that the foam is concealed, and that all the materials are secured. Finally, mist spray the design.

ALTERNATIVE FLOWER CHOICE
For focal flowers you could use Dendrobium orchids or double-headed Eustoma, and for filler flowers Convallaria, spray Dianthus, spray Chrysanthemum, Solidaster, Mimosa, Astilbe.

Alternative small foliages would be Rosmarinus officinalis (rosemary), Buxus sempervirens (box), Pittosporum tenufolium.

Bridal Posy with Fancy Frame

This design is created in a bridal belle holder.

MATERIALS
Fresh flowers and foliages
One Eucalyptus parvifolia
Two Gypsophila 'Million Star' (filler flowers)
Twelve Rosa 'Joy' (focal flowers)

Sundries
Bridal holder with wet foam
Decorative ribbon and silk ivy leaves; double-sided tape
Decorative aluminium wire, silver and pink
Beaded garland
Decorative headed pins
Florist's knife and scissors

SUITABILITY
This design is suitable for a bridesmaid's posy as much as for the bride; for a civil service ceremony; or as a presentation bouquet. A nice touch is to cover the bridal holder with cord/ribbon/silk petals/fresh leaves/spray in colours that match and complement the colours of the wedding.

Storage (florist)
Store this design upright and in the dark; keep it cool, and spray when needed. For transport and delivery, use the following method: cover a lidded box with paper, cut a hole in the lid and then insert the finished bouquet into the hole so that it sits flush with the box.

Care (customer)
Store the bouquet out of direct sunlight and heat until you are ready to use it; handle with care.

METHOD
1. Stick double-sided tape down the handle, and wind the ribbon on to the holder – starting at the base, wind it along the handle, keeping the tension on the ribbon or cord. Next use double-sided tape to stick some artificial ivy leaves round the base of the holder. You could always use fresh leaves – however, this could not be prepared in advance. To finish the holder décor, cover over the 'join' where the ribbon and ivy

1. Prepare the holder handle.

2. Make an aluminium wire frame.

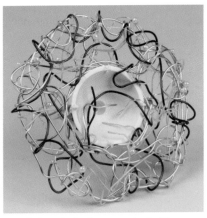

3. Attach the frame to the holder.

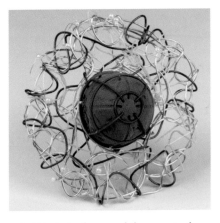

4. Attach the foam and the cage to the design.

5. Insert the foliages and Gypsophila.

6. Insert the Rosa, spacing them equally round the design.

leaves meet the aluminium wire.

2. Start to make the decorative wire frame: the construction method is similar to finger crochet. First make about six to eight loops. Push the first wire loop through the next loop and bend it over, then move to the next loop, and so on – and once you have 'crocheted' all the way around, repeat the process with the next outer loops. Continue with this method until you have created a pleasing posy (a round shape).

3. Thread a different-coloured wire through this mesh posy, and attach the wire posy to the holder: remove the foam and cage and push the mesh into the holder, keeping the attaching clips free.

4. Carefully replace the foam into the prepared holder and clip the cage firmly back on over the clips of the holder. Now dunk the foam briefly into a bucket (being careful not to get the ribbon wet), for five seconds only – any longer

and the foam could disintegrate and water drip down the customer's dress.

5. Cut Eucalyptus foliage to a similar size and insert it into the foam, creating a slightly domed profile – do not let it extend over the prepared frame. The next step is to cut the Gypsophila into small pieces and insert it into the foam, being careful to give an even coverage.

6. Cut and add the roses into the holder – they should be long enough to have a

7. As an extra option you could add decorative wire.

slightly higher profile than the eucalyptus, and should be spaced evenly round the design.

7. As an optional finish you could push some decorative headed pins into the top of the roses, and loosely bind a beaded garland over the finished design.

8. Finally check that the frame is held securely to the holder, that all the materials are secure and none is damaged, and that the foam is concealed. Spray with water.

ALTERNATIVE MATERIALS
For flowers you could use spray Chrysanthemum or spray Dianthus, and Chamelaucium (wax flower), Limonium and Solidaster as fillers.
Small foliages could include Rosmarinus

officinalis (rosemary), Buxus sempervirens (box), Myrtus communis (myrtle), and Pittosporum tenufolium.

······································

Wired Designs

Standard Buttonhole

This project describes how to create a standard buttonhole with a stem.

MATERIALS
Fresh flowers and foliages
One Dianthus 'Prado'
Five Hedera leaves

Sundries
Headed pin
32m-gauge reel wire
71mm wire

Floral tape
Scissors

SUITABILITY
This buttonhole is suitable for a variety of formal occasions: prom celebrations, weddings – for the groom, the father of the bride, the best man, the father of the groom, ushers, key guests – and civil weddings; also for formal ceremonies, and occasions such as Ascot horse races. It is to be worn on the lapel, attached by a headed pin.

Storage (florist)
This buttonhole should be prepared as near as possible to the event. Once made, spray it, and store in a dark and cool place. The advantage of leaving the stem on is that it will help to retain maximum moisture for the flower head. For transportation, put the buttonhole in a prepared box with a cellophane cover; ensure that the headed pin is inserted into the stem ready for attachment by the customer.

Care (customer)
Keep the buttonhole in a cool, dark place until ready for wear; then pin it on to the left lapel, stem down, with the pin provided.

1. Branching unit of three leaves.

METHOD

1. Using 32mm-gauge reel wire, support wire five ivy leaves using the stitched method; then tape the wires. Create a branching unit out of three leaves (the top one must be smaller); this unit strengthens the leaves.

2. Look at the Dianthus to see if it has a natural 'front' (it could have a slight tilt to the head), then support wire it using the external method. First tape a 71mm-gauge wire, but leaving the top bit untaped. Poke the untaped wire into the calyx at the 'back' of the Dianthus, then twist the wire twice round the stem, once above and once below the node.

3. Using the reel wire, bind the pre-made branching unit just under the calyx head, putting the unit at the back of the design – this obscures the support wiring method. Do not cut the binding wire.

4. Lay two pre-stitched ivy leaves against the front of the Dianthus, facing the leaves inwards so the front of the leaves are touching the Dianthus – this will form the front of the buttonhole; using the binding wire, bind them on over the same binding point.

5. Cut the binding wire, and tape over the binding point and down the stem. Pull the front two leaves down to conceal the binding area – this is called 'facing'. Cut the stem so that it is 6.5cm (2.5in) long, and attach the pin to the stem. Be careful not to put the pin all the way through the stem – this ensures that the customer will not prick themselves when removing the buttonhole from the presentation box.

6. Carry out your routine quality checks: check the flower for damage, and remove any damaged petals; ensure that there are no sharp wires, that the binding point is covered, and that the pin is attached. Spray with water.

Professional tip: If a number of buttonholes are prepared the day before their requirement, do not cut the stems but leave them long and put them into water – then on the day of delivery/collection, cut the stems, dry them off and tape the ends so they retain as much moisture as possible and so keep looking fresh.

ALTERNATIVE FLOWER CHOICE
The following flowers could also be used for this buttonhole as an alternative to Dianthus: Rosa, Erynigum, Phalaenopsis orchid, Cymbidium orchid. The following foliages could be used as an alternative: hard Ruscus, Gaultheria shallon (Salal), Galax leaves.

Non-Standard Buttonhole

This project describes how to create a non-standard buttonhole, with no stem.

MATERIALS
Fresh flowers and foliages
One Rosa 'Sphinx'
Five Hedera leaves
Two strands Liriope gigantea (lily grass)

Sundries
Headed pin
52mm-gauge reel wire
71mm wire
46mm wire
Floral tape
Scissors
Secateurs

3. Bind the branching unit on to the stem.

2. External wire support.

5. The finished buttonhole.

4. Face and bind on the front Hedera leaves.

SUITABILITY

This buttonhole is suitable for a variety of formal occasions: prom celebrations, weddings – for the groom, the father of the bride, the best man, the father of the groom, ushers, key guests – and civil weddings; also for occasions such as Ascot horse races. It is to be worn on the lapel, attached by the headed pin provided.

The advantage of a non-standard buttonhole without a natural stem over one with a stem is that it is lighter and less bulky, and therefore more elegant, and so could be worn by a woman, such as the mother of the bride or the best lady.

Storage (florist)

This buttonhole should be prepared as near as possible to the event. Once made, spray it, and store in a dark and cool place. For transportation, put the buttonhole in a prepared box with a cellophane cover; ensure that the headed pin is inserted into the stem ready for attachment by the customer.

Care (customer)

Keep the buttonhole in a cool, dark place until ready for wear; then pin it on to the left lapel, stem down, with the pin provided.

METHOD

The method of construction is basically the same as for the standard buttonhole, but with the following differences in Step 1:

1. Prepare the Rosa by removing the stem – though be careful not to cut it too short, or taping will be very difficult – and support wire it using a cross-stitched method: first insert 71mm-gauge wire into the stem, then thread 46mm-gauge wire across the stem horizontally – pull this wire down on each side of the first wire so you have three wires parallel to each other; then tape it round, making sure that the stem end is covered to keep in the moisture.

1. Cross stitch the Rosa head.

2. The branching unit of three leaves.

3. Bind the branching unit onto the stem.

4. Add the wired loop of grass.

5. Face and bind on the two front Hedera leaves.

6. The finished design.

Then repeat the same construction steps as for the standard buttonhole.

Wired Corsage, Line Style

This project describes how to create a wired corsage, line style.

MATERIALS
Fresh flowers and foliages
Six heads of a spray Rosa 'Fireflash'
One Genista
Hedera helix

Sundries
Floral tape
32-gauge reel wire
70mm wire

SUITABILITY

This design is suitable for formal occasions such as prom celebrations and weddings – for the mother of the bride, for the grandmothers, the best lady, for key lady guests – for civil ceremonies, Ascot horse races, or other special days. It is to be worn on clothing, made secure by the headed pin provided. If attached to a floral magnet it could be pinned to a handbag or to a hat; and if attached to a hair comb it could be worn in the hair (see Wired Hair Comb).

Storage (florist)

This design should be prepared as near as possible to the event. Once made, spray it, and store in a dark and cool place. For transportation, put the design in a prepared box with a cellophane cover.

Care (customer)

Keep the corsage in a cool, dark place until ready for wear; then pin it onto the left lapel, stems up, with the pin provided.

METHOD

1. This design has the proportions of one-third to two-thirds, so ensure that enough flowers are wired up by laying them out on your workbench as a guide.

2. Support wire the Rosas (the focal flowers) with the pipping method, the Genista using the single leg method, and two branching units of two ivy leaves (see Wiring Techniques at the beginning of this chapter). Start with one of the branching units: layer the prepared ivy leaves so they form a triangular shape, being careful not to overlap the leaves too much, but not leaving any gaps, either; then bind the leaves together with 32mm-gauge reel wire, keeping the binding wire in one area only. Do not cut the binding wire.

3. Slot in the Rosas between the ivy leaves – start off with the smallest head, and

1. Sort out the flowers needed for the design.

2. Create a triangle of Hedera leaves.

3. Insert the first Rosa.

4. Insert the second Rosa.

5. Insert the third Rosa.

6. Insert the fourth Rosa.

7. Create a smaller triangle of Hedera leaves.

8. Face the Hedera leaves to create a return end.

9. Bind on the return end.

10. Insert the fifth Rosa.

11. Insert the sixth Rosa.

12. The binding point.

13. Trim the stems.

14. Profile view.

15. The finished design.

add a wired piece of Genista; bind these into the corsage.

4. Add the second Rosa – stagger it slightly off centre to the left, and bind it in.

5. Add the third Rosa – stagger it slightly off centre to the right, and bind it in.

6. Add the largest, focal Rosa with another wired piece of Genista, and bind these in.

7. Start the 'return' end of the ivy leaves – you are aiming to create a smaller ivy triangle, half the size of the first ivy triangle (this is the one-third to two-third proportion).

8. Face the first ivy leaf so that the right side of the leaf touches the focal flower: bind it in and bend it back – the wire has an L-shaped profile.

9. Put the remaining leaves into position, always binding them in at the same binding point so that it doesn't travel.

10. Insert the fifth Rosa in the return end, in a staggered line with the others.

11. Insert the last Rosa (a small head) and a wired piece of Genista so they lie within the leaf outline.

12. The binding point should remain in one place.

13. Trim off the excess wires, then tape over the binding point wires and down the 'stem'.

14. Adjust the materials so that you achieve a pleasing profile, making sure that the focal flower is proud of the others.

15. The final outline resembles a kite shape.

16. Check that all the wires are safely taped in, and that there is no damage to any of the materials. Spray the design, and add a decorative pin for the customer to secure the corsage to the garment.

ALTERNATIVES

One option is to create different outline shapes, such as a crescent, posy, or extended; or use different materials, always considering their longevity.

Alternative focal flowers might include Orchids, spray Chrysanthemums, spray Dianthus. Filler alternatives could be Chamelaucium, Solidaster, Limonium.

Wired Corsage, Posy Style

This project describes how to create a wired corsage, posy style.

MATERIALS
Fresh flowers and foliages
Six heads of a spray Rosa 'Glorious'
Eight Hedera helix

Sundries
Floral tape
32-gauge reel wire
70mm wire
Headed pin

SUITABILITY
This design is suitable for formal occasions such as prom celebrations and weddings – for the mother of the bride, for the grandmothers, the best lady, for key lady guests – for civil ceremonies, Ascot horse races, or other special days. It is to be worn on clothing, made secure by the headed pin provided. If attached to a floral magnet it could be pinned to a handbag or to a hat; and if attached to a hair comb it could be worn in the hair (see Wired Hair Comb).

Storage (florist)
This design should be prepared as near as possible to the event. Once made, spray it, and store in a dark and cool place. For transportation, put the posy in a prepared box with a cellophane cover.

Care (customer)
Keep the corsage in a cool, dark place until ready for wear; then pin it onto the left lapel, stems down, with the pin provided.

METHOD
1. Choose five Hedera helix leaves of identical size. When selecting the leaves, ensure that their size is correct for the design and the selected flowers: leaves that are too big will make the flowers look inadequate; too small, and the flowers will look an untidy mess. Also, always work in numbers over four: this is because four leaves form a square and therefore a posy outline will be impossible to achieve. Stitch support wire and tape the chosen leaves (see Wiring Techniques for guidance). Bundle the five outer leaves together, then pull them out to create a posy to determine the binding point; the leaves should gently touch, with no gaps between them. Bind using 32-gauge wire (do not cut the wire).

2. Support wire the Rosa heads, and tape them using the 'pipping' method (see Wiring Techniques). Place one rose into the core of the design to determine the right height, then bend the flower head over so that it rests on the ivy leaf – its ideal position is to sit at the base of the ivy so that you can still see the leaf.

3. Once you have achieved the correct placement, insert the remainder of the outer roses into the core at the same height as the measured one; then bind them into position.

4. Bend all the outer ring roses into position, and insert any optional accessories such as beads or feathers.

1. The outer ring of Hedera leaves.

2. Gauging the height of the Rosa.

3. Add all the outer Rosa.

4. The outer Rosa faced with added decorative beads.

7. Bind the posy.

8. Face the posy for ease of wear.

5. Add the inner Hedera leaves.

6. Add the focal Rosa.

9. The finished design.

5. Add the inner, smaller ivy leaves, binding them in at the original binding point– these conceal the mechanics of the corsage.

6. Insert the central focal rose, being careful not to place it too high or it will be too proud, nor too snug and low into the design; bind it in securely.

7. The binding point should be kept in one place.

8. Cut off the excess wires, and tape over the binding point and down the 'stem'. Then start to 'face' the design so that it can be worn – the aim being that the 'stem' of the posy touches the bottom leaves and roses: bend and face the whole design.

9. Bend over all the components of the design.

10. Quality check: ensure that all the wires are safely taped in, and that there is no damage to materials. Spray the design, and add a decorative pin for the customer to secure the posy to their garment.

Wired Bridal Posy

Wired bouquets have the following advantages: you can make them to any desired outline shape, they are light to hold, and if well made, the materials are very secure. Some flowers will not insert into a foam holder because the stems are too large or too soft. The featured design cannot be constructed using a foam holder because the stems of the flowers cut from a stem of orchids would not be long enough. A disadvantage of wired bridal work is that wired flowers will not last long out of water.

MATERIALS
Fresh flowers and foliages
Two Aspidistra leaves
Two stems of mini Cymbidium orchids

Sundries
Floral tape
Assorted wires
32-gauge reel wire
Ribbon
Skeletonized leaves
Diamante, beaded picks

SUITABILITY
This posy is suitable for a bridesmaid or for the bride herself, for a civil service ceremony or as a presentation bouquet.

Storage (florist)
This design should be prepared as near as possible to the event. Once made, store it in a dark and cool place where there is no risk of it being crushed; spray when necessary. For transport and delivery, cover a lidded box with paper, cut a hole in the lid and then insert the finished bouquet into the hole so that it sits flush with the box.

Care (customer)
Store the posy out of direct sunlight and heat until ready for use; handle with care.

METHOD
1. Support and mount wire the orchid heads (using the cross-stitched support method and single leg mount wire method) and the aspidistra loops (strip the aspidistra into thin strips and mount wire with the single leg mount method); stitch the skeletonized leaves with decorative wire (see the Wiring Techniques section at the beginning of this chapter for guidance). Start to form a posy shape centre by using a large orchid and add three skeletonized leaves, three picks and three striped Aspidistra leaves; bind all these together.

1. Bind the prepared materials to create the centre core of the design.

2. Continue to add materials.

3. Add a collar of skeletonized leaves.

4. Tape the handle, and tape the bow to the top of the handle.

5. Create the ribbon handle.

2. Continue to add materials round the centre flower, 'facing' the orchid heads inwards and ensuring a round outline shape, and keeping it visually balanced with the equal use of skeletonized and Aspidistra leaves. Keep to the original binding point.

3. Once all the fresh materials are inserted into the design, add a collar of stitched skeletonized leaves round the edge of the design to frame the posy. Bind over the binding point and tape down the stem.

4. This will create the handle: the optimum length should be 14cm (from the binding point), so cut it to this length but leaving one wire 5cm longer than the rest. The ribbon handle finish is very elegant but this should be the last job to be done before delivery (if a flower has died it is easily replaceable, but once the ribbon is completely on, it makes it more time consuming). Tie a single bow, and tie a wire round the middle which you can then tape to the handle.

5. Start the ribboning – leave about 10cm of ribbon 'tuck' behind the bow – this gives some tension to the ribbon, which helps when you twist it round the handle. Ribbon down the handle until you reach the single wire that is sticking out at the bottom; twist the ribbon around this a couple of turns, then bend

6. The finished design.

the wire up and carry the ribbon back up the handle, keeping the tension on as you do so. Once back at the bow at the top, cut off the ribbon end leaving enough to tie to the starting ribbon that you tucked behind the bow. Tie once above and once below the bow to secure it, and cut to the desired length.

6. Check that all the material is secure, that no sharp wires are protruding, and that there is no damage to the flowers; then mist the design.

....

Headwear Requirements

There are various designs that a florist can suggest for wedding ceremonies; fashion dictates some of the choices, but flower choice is also important. The following points should be considered when choosing flora and taking headwear orders:

Seasonal availability: Check that the chosen flower is available on the wedding date.

Scale/size of the flower head: Think of the scale of the design – that for a floral headpiece for an adult bride or bridesmaid would be different to that required for a four-year-old bridesmaid. Small round flowers and leaves are usually suitable – for example spray roses, Chamelaucium, spray Dianthus, spray Chrysanthemum.

Durability out of water: As the head is very warm, durability is doubly important because the stems are removed and suitable wiring techniques applied to the flower. Unsuitable flowers would be Lathyrus (sweet pea) and Eustoma.

Thorns: Any thorns would need to be removed, if possible – for example from Rosa – but some materials would be just too prickly, for example Ilex (holly leaves), Eryngium.

Pollen: Avoid using flowers that contain a lot of pollen; this could be especially important if the wearer suffers from hay fever or allergies.

Toxic: Avoid using flora that could be toxic to the wearer, especially young bridesmaids, who are more likely to touch and fiddle! One flora that falls into this category is Aconitum.

Head sizing: Good fit is essential – head sizes are like dress sizes: we are all different – so getting the correct measurement is important in order for the design to look good and feel comfortable to wear.

Hair colouring: If you have three bridesmaids with different hair colours – for instance blonde, copper and dark brown – flower colour choice would be key. In this circumstance you might offer the same choice of design and flower but in different colours.

Wired Circlet

MATERIALS
Fresh flowers and foliages
Eight Muscari heads
Eight spray Rosa heads
One stem of Pittosporum tenufolium
Eight Hedera helix leaves
One Gypsophila

Sundries
Eight beaded picks

90-/71-/56-/46-/32-gauge wires
Tape
Scissors

SUITABILITY
This circlet is suitable for young bridesmaids at a wedding, for young people going to a pop festival, for holy communion ceremonies.

Storage (florist)
This design should be prepared as near as

2. Tape on the first part of the pattern.

3. Tape on the second part of the pattern.

4. Keep taping on the materials.

5. Check that the pattern fits.

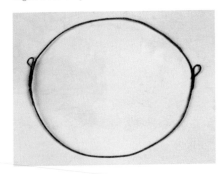

1. Stay wire with hair attachments.

6. The finished design.

possible to the event. Once made, spray it, and store it in a dark and cool place. Transport circlets in a lidded box of appropriate size; if preparing more than one circlet, add a named label to each one to ensure that each wearer gets the correct head size.

Care (customer)
Keep the circlet in a cool, dark place until ready for wear.

METHOD
1. Tape two 90mm-gauge wires together to make a longer wire. Once the head size has been determined, cut the prepared wire 4cm longer than needed. Join both ends together so that they overlap by 2cm at each end (by overlapping by this amount the circle of wire will fit the required head size): this circle becomes the stay wire. Create two hair attachments: first tape a 56mm wire, then cut it into two small pieces, and tape both pieces on to the prepared circle stay wire.

2. Lay out the flowers and foliages in a line and in a repeat pattern to the required head size, making sure that you have enough to complete the design for that particular size. The pictured example has a repeat pattern of two sequences:

   a) Ivy leaf/spray Rosa/gypsophila
   b) Pittosporum/muscari/beaded pick

   Support wire all the elements as appropriate:

   For a): Ivy leaf – stitch with 32mm-gauge reel wire
   Rosa – pip with 46mm-gauge reel wire
   Gypsophila – use a 56mm-gauge natural unit

   For b): Pittosporum – use a 56mm-gauge single leg mount
   Muscari – use 32mm-gauge cross stitch

(be careful of these stems as they are very soft)
Beaded picks – these have their own wires

These wire weights are only meant as a guide, and will not always be appropriate – stems and flower heads vary in size and weight, so use the appropriate weight of wires according to the stems.
   Start to tape on the flowers – if using Stemtex (registered trademark) use half-width tape to minimize the weight and visual bulk – layering and spacing according to the sequence of the pattern: start with the ivy leaf/spray Rosa/Gypsophila.

3. Then add the next sequence pattern – Pittosporum, Muscari and beaded pick.

4. Keep taping on the prepared materials, being careful not to tape over the hair attachment loops, but taping round them.

5. When you have nearly worked all the way round the stay wire, check that your patterns will 'fit' into the remaining space, and if necessary 'tweak' the spacing accordingly.

6. Once you have worked all the way round the circlet do not cut the wires as this will make the last few taped items very insecure, but continue to tape the wires until both ends are concealed, weaving the tape between the flowers that are already taped on.

7. Finally carry out your routine quality checks: ensure that no materials are damaged and that all are secure on the stay wire; also that no wires are protruding and all are concealed. Adjust the materials so that when the circlet is being worn all flower heads are facing to the outside. Mist spray the

finished design.

ALTERNATIVE FLOWERS
Alternative materials that can be used are as follows: for focal flowers Hyacinthus, Stephanotis florets; for filler flowers wax flower, Limonium; for leaves Ruscus, Galax.

Wired Alice Band
MATERIALS
Fresh flowers and foliages
Hedera (Ivy leaves)
Blue hyacinth
White hyacinth
Viburnum

Sundries
Assorted wires
Tape
Coloured wire
Beads

SUITABILITY
The Alice band or half circlet is normally worn from ear to ear across the top of the head; smaller versions can be worn under a hair bun or on a side chignon hair design. At the time of writing it is fashionable for younger bridesmaids to wear this style of design.

Storage (florist)
This design should be prepared as near as possible to the event. Once made, spray it, and store in a dark and cool place. Transport the design in a lidded box of appropriate size.

Care (customer)
Keep in a cool, dark place until ready for wear.

METHOD
1. Tape two 90mm-gauge wires: these will form the stay wires on which the ribbed units will be formed. The customer measurement is taken from ear to ear over the top of the head: by halving this

measurement you can work out the amount of materials required for each stay wire. Then lay out the pattern of chosen foliages (Hedera): this will be a symmetric design, so each line of Hedera leaves must be equal.

2. Support wire the materials: first the hyacinth with the pipped technique using a decorative wire with a beaded finish (see photograph) – although the pipped technique can be achieved without the bead. Then single leg mount the viburnum with a 32mm-gauge wire. Using half-width tape, tape the prepared materials – tape only a couple of centimetres, just enough to cover the end of the stem and the manipulated wires.

3. Start to tape on the prepared Hedera leaves – start at the end of the taped 90mm gauge so that the leaf is level with the taped stay wire.

4. Tape on the prepared flowers – where the flowers and foliages are mixed this is known as a 'ribbed unit'.

5. Continue to tape the materials to the ribbed unit until you have completed a third of the overall measurement; then make the other ribbed unit identical to the first.

6. On one of the ribbed units create a focal area (this part of the Alice band will be positioned on the top of the head).

7. Once the focal area is complete, cut both ribbed units so that you have 4cm at both ends; then tape these.

8. Line up both ends and tape them carefully together, weaving the tape between the flowers so that no uncovered wire ends can be seen, and so there are no gaps.

1. Prepare the stay wires and the materials.

2. Pip the hyacinth heads.

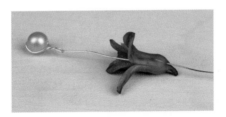

3. Tape the wired leaf to the stay wire.

4. Tape on the flowers.

5. Two identical ribbed units.

6. Create a focal area on one of the ribbed units.

7. Cut and tape the unit ends.

9. The ribbed unit is now complete.

10. Carefully bend the ribbed unit into a crescent shape so that it will fit comfortably on a head.

11. Make your quality checks: ensure that no materials are damaged, and that all materials are secure on the stay wire; also that no wires are protruding, and all are concealed. Adjust the materials so that when the Alice band is being worn all are facing to the outside. Mist spray the finished design.

8. Attach the units together.

9. Front view of the unit.

ALTERNATIVE FLOWERS
Flower choice: spray roses, Dendrobium orchids.
Filler flowers: gypsophila, Chamelaucium (wax flower).
Foliage: hard Ruscus.

Wired Hair Comb
MATERIALS
Fresh flowers and foliages
Assorted Hedera helix (ivy leaves)
Four mini Cymbidium heads
One Sedum
Four stems of Liriope gigantea (lily grass)

Sundries
Assorted wires
Floral tape
Feathers
Hair comb
Thin satin ribbon

SUITABILITY
This is a hair design that could be used instead of a veil for a bride – if the bride were getting married overseas, or for a tropical wedding theme, a civil ceremony or for a mature bride. It is suitable for long hair, and can be worn to the side or at the back of the head depending on the hair style – so this aspect would have to be discussed with the customer. It is more suitable for the adult bridesmaid, although

10. The shaped and finished Alice band.

smaller versions could be constructed for a younger bridesmaid. It could be worn for a formal function, or instead of a hat at a formal occasion.

Storage (florist)
Keep the design in a cool, dark place; mist spray when necessary. To transport the hair comb, put it in a prepared box with a cellophane cover.

Care (customer)
Keep the design in a cool, dark place until the wearer is ready to put it on; be very careful not to crush it.

METHOD
1. Support wire and tape the chosen materials: stitch the ivy leaves; single leg mount the Sedum, grass and feathers, and cross stitch the orchid heads (see Wiring Techniques at the beginning of this chapter for guidance). Wire weight depends on the thickness of the stem – to check, apply the 'bounce' test. Always try and use the lightest wire possible so the design does not become heavy to wear.

2. Construct the hair comb using the same technique as the line corsage, with a

'return end' with one binding point. Create the outline shape with ivy leaves – a small triangle – then add into the corsage a staggered line of orchid

1. Tape and wire the materials.

2. Construct one end of the design.

3. Construct the return end of the design; cut the wires.

4. The binding point.

5. Attach the design to the comb with binding wire.

6. Cover the wire attachment with the ribbon.

7. The finished design.

heads, interspersed with Sedum, feathers and loops of grass. Bind under the second orchid: this will become the binding point.

3. Complete the 'return end': reverse the material order, staggering the orchid heads, Sedum, feathers and Hedera leaves, inserting and binding in as you go. Cut the stems: they should be short enough to be concealed by the corsage.

4. Tape over the binding point and down the stem.

5. Using the 32mm-gauge binding wire, bind the design firmly onto the hair comb.

6. Cover the binding wire attachment with thin satin ribbon: wind the ribbon round the whole length of the comb for added security and to give a professional finish (as an alternative you could use floral tape instead of ribbon).

7. Check that all the materials are damage free and secure, that there are no sharp wires, and that all the wiring is concealed. Spray the design.

ALTERNATIVE IDEAS

The corsage could be attached to a different kind of hair accessory, for example a hair band, or a quick-release hair clip. For guidance as to flower choice, see Headwear Requirements at the beginning of this section.

Glued Wedding Techniques

There are two main glues that can help the florist to create floral designs: hot glue and cold floral glue.

Hot glue: A stick of glue is inserted into the glue gun holder, which heats it up to 170°C – so care is needed when handling this tool – and even more so if it is an electric gun, where all the risks of using electricity around the workshop apply. Always use the glue gun stand, work on a non-flammable mat or tile, do not force the glue sticks into the gun, and avoid contact with the hot adhesive – if it contacts the skin, treat it as a burn. Allow the gun to cool fully before putting it away – do not touch the glue nozzle for about 30 minutes after switching off!

Despite the obvious risks in using this product, it is a great glue to use when extra bonding is required – and due to its nature it can cope with heavy duty gluing needs. Do not use on fresh products, as it will burn and scald them. Glue sticks are available in different colours, and in gold and silver glitter – great for contemporary work – where the glue is intended to be seen.

Cold floral glue: This is a clear glue that is waterproof and will not mark petals or foliages. Add a blob of glue to both of the sides that require bonding; allow it to go tacky, then fasten together.

Glued Corsage

MATERIALS
Fresh flowers and foliages
One stem Ornithogalum thyrsoides (two heads) (focal flower)
One stem Convallaria (lily of the valley)
Three Liriope muscari (china grass)
Two Galax leaves

Sundries
Hessian-backed birch
One corsage magnet
Assorted beads
Skeletonized leaves
Floristry glue

SUITABILITY
This is an alternative version to the traditional corsage worn on the lapel of a jacket or dress. This design has a contemporary feel, and can be worn at formal occasions, at weddings, by both partners at a civil wedding, or for prom celebrations; with a name added it could be used as a conference badge. This particular design is attached by a floral magnet, and it is important to be aware that the magnet could interfere with a pacemaker, so you do need to check that the recipient is aware of this – if this is the case you can substitute with a different fitting, such as a broach.

Storage (florist)
Store in dark, cool area until delivery or collection, and mist according to the materials used. For transportation, put the design in a prepared box with a cellophane cover.

Care (customer)
Avoid placing the design in direct sunlight; attach it to the lapel using the magnet.

METHOD
1. Cut a piece of hessian-backed birch, or replace this with an alternative backing. Glue half the floral magnet on to the back of a Galax leaf.

2. Stick the leaf firmly on the back of the birch, and then glue the second half of the magnet to the other side of the leaf – this layering of the leaf between the magnet helps the customer ease the magnets apart.

3. Turn the birch over so it is the right side up. Stick skeleton leaves on to it, taking great care not to over-use the glue as it will leave marks that it will not be possible to remove. Stick the Galax leaf next – by layering many colours and textures a greater visual interest is created.

4. Stick the china grass strips and a double layer of Ornithogalum floret heads on to the corsage.

5. Finish the corsage by sticking the beads

1. Glue the magnet on to the backing.

2. Layer the magnet between the leaf and the backing.

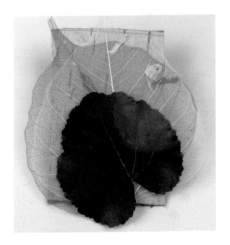

3. Glue on the layer of leaves.

4. Glue on the flowers.

and the Convallaria heads on to the design.

6. Check that all the materials are firmly attached, and that there are no sharp edges.

ALTERNATIVE FLOWER/FOLIAGE
An alternative for the badge backing might be a large leaf such as Hedera, a Camilla leaf, Gaultheria shallon, pressed sisal, or pressed moulded decorative wires.

An alternative flower choice might be from amongst any long-lasting small flowers, for example Stephanotis, Hypericum berries, a hydrangea floret, a small spray Rosa, Ornithogalum

5. The finished corsage.

saundersiae florets, Limonium, or a Hyacinthus floret.

A fixture alternative could be a badge, a broach or a T-bar.

Glued Alice Band

The technique of gluing has many advantages, but in particular speed of construction – especially useful if there are many designs to produce for one function; also it can help create a very full design using many flowers. Its disadvantages are that the flowers chosen must tolerate being out of water, and it is difficult not to transfer glue to the front of the materials. Small, textured materials work well because they enable layering of the design – but it is important still to apply the elements and principles of design when choosing them.

MATERIALS
Fresh flowers and foliages
Seven spray Rosa heads
One stem Gypsophila 'My Pink'
Ten Lavandula (lavender)
Assorted size Hedera leaves from small to medium

Sundries
Clear Alice band
Floral glue

SUITABILITY
An Alice band or a half circlet is normally worn from ear to ear across the top of the head; smaller versions can be worn under a hair bun or on a side chignon hair design. At the time of writing it is fashionable for younger bridesmaids to wear this style of design; it could also be worn for Holy Communion services. Make sure before constructing it that the band fits correctly.

Storage (florist)

Store in a dark, cool area until delivery or collection, and mist according to the materials used. Transport in a lidded box of an appropriate size.

1. Prepare the materials and add the glue.

3. Start to stick on the materials at both ends of the band.

Care (customer)

It is important to advise the customer on how to wear the design – the position on the wearer's head is important.

2. Continue to stick on the materials.

4. The finished band.

5. The finished band being worn.

METHOD

1. Select and grade your chosen flowers, removing all the stems so that the materials can be glued flush to the band. Once you have completed this process, apply a blob of glue to the reverse – you will need to work fairly rapidly once you have applied the glue.

2. Once the glue becomes tacky, stick on the materials, working from the tips of the band – apply the materials in turn to each side to maintain a symmetric design, taking care to use the same sized materials on both sides: start with the smaller flowers at the ends of the band, and larger ones in the centre.

3. Continue gluing the materials along each side of the band.

4. Complete this process until the whole band is concealed, finishing at the centre at the top of the band with a larger Rosa, being careful not to make it too proud.

5. Spray the design generously. Check that all the materials are firmly stuck on to the band, and that when held upright there are no 'gaps' between the band and the flowers.

ALTERNATIVE IDEAS

Other flowers could be used, for example Dendrobium orchids; however, be careful in the choice of flowers because not only do they need to tolerate being out of water, but the profile needs to be compact. You could use massed flowers of one type only, for example Hyacinthus florets.

....

Wrist Corsages

Wristlets are an increasingly popular design due to prom functions, but now that people are aware of this design it is often requested for weddings and other formal functions. There are many different products on the market that cater for the demand: flexi bands can fit any size and are available in different colours, and corsage designs can be glued direct on to these, or wired corsages attached to them; there are diamante and beaded bracelets where again the corsage designs can be either wired or glued on; or self-made bangles of soft aluminium wire that can be moulded around the arm. Another method is a ribbon tied around the wrist where the corsage requires sewing on to this.

Considerations regarding flower choice are similar to those relevant to head designs (see Headwear Requirements at the beginning of this section for guidance). In addition the profile should be considered, because if the focal flower is too high it can look comical and is easily knocked off. Artificial flowers are a good alternative, and their use means that the whole design can be kept as a keepsake reminder of the special occasion.

Wrist Corsage, Glued Design

The technique of gluing has many advantages, in particular the speed of construction – this is especially useful if many designs are needed for one function; it can also be used to create a variety of styles both contemporary and traditional. One of gluing's disadvantages is that the flowers chosen must tolerate being out of water; also it is difficult not to transfer glue to the front of the plant material. This wrist corsage is designed using a flexi-band shimmer wrap.

MATERIALS
Fresh flowers and foliages
Two spray Rosa heads 'Viviane'
Two Liriope muscari (china grass)
Four Senecio leaves of various sizes

Sundries
Floral glue
Floral glitter

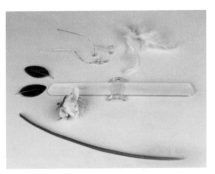

1. Prepare the materials.

2. Start to glue on the base layers.

3. Glue on the focal flower.

4. The finished design.

Diamante picks
A few cream feathers
Wristlet – shimmer wrap

SUITABILITY
This wrist corsage is suitable for bridesmaids, prom celebrations, formal dinner functions and parties.

Storage (florist)
Store in a dark, cool place, and mist as necessary. Place in a special corsage box before collection/ delivery.

Care (customer)
Store the corsage in a dark, cool place until it is needed; be very careful not to crush it.

METHOD
1. Prepare all the components by cutting off all the stems of foliage, even at the back of the rose so that it lies flat. Choose accessories appropriate to the customer – the featured design is suitable for a prom celebration so feathers, glitter and diamante picks are appropriate. Before gluing the materials into position, check the centre of the band on your wrist and mark the band so you know where to start gluing.

2. Put a small amount of glue on the back of the foliage, Rosa, accessories and band: allow the glue to become tacky. Quickly and carefully layer the materials, taking care not to transfer the glue on to any visible areas. Start the design with the bottom layer. For the best effect, use contrasting textures next to each other, such as matt velvety leaves next to shiny grass and fluffy feathers.

3. Next, stick the focal rose flower onto the band, but before doing so, stick a circle of rose petals round the base of the main rose and slightly larger than the main rose, to improve its size without increasing its profile – which would make it difficult for the wearer

and potentially get knocked off. Once all is secure, spray the design with a fine layer of floral glue and sprinkle on glitter.

4. Check that all the materials are securely stuck to the band. Mist carefully, taking care not to spray the material-covered band, which could mark.

1. Support wire and tape the materials.

2. Construct one end of the corsage.

3. Construct the 'return' end of the corsage.

Wrist Corsage, Wired Design
Using the technique of wiring, the florist can create different outline shapes in a way that might not be possible using just glue.

This corsage is designed on a diamante bracelet (a rock bracelet).

MATERIALS
Fresh flowers and foliages
Two small Phalaenopsis orchid flower head
Seven assorted Hedera helix leaves

4. Attach to the band.

5. The finished design.

Sundries
Two feathers
One diamante wrist bracelet
A small piece of aluminium wire
Ribbon
Diamante sticky dots
Assorted floral wires
Floral tape

SUITABILITY
This wrist corsage is suitable for bridesmaids, prom celebrations, formal dinner functions, parties.

Storage (florist)
Store the wrist corsage in a dark, cool place, and mist as necessary. Place it in a special corsage box before collection/delivery.

Care (customer)
Store the corsage in a dark, cool place until it is needed; be very careful not to crush it.

METHOD
1. Support wire all the fresh materials and accessories, and tape neatly. The following techniques should be used: for the ivy – stitch; for the orchid – cross stitch; and for the feathers – single leg mount (see Wiring Techniques at the beginning of this chapter for guidance). The wire weight selected will depend on the thickness of the stem – to check, apply the bounce test. Always try and use the lightest wire possible so that the design does not become heavy to wear.

2. Construct the design using the same technique as a corsage, starting at one end with a branching unit of two Hedera helix: this will support the orchid head. Then layer in the feathers and curled ribbon, and then the orchid head, and bind tightly below the orchid head. Keep the design small or it will be out of scale with the wearer's wrist.

3. Now construct the 'return' end of the corsage by reversing the material order, inserting and binding in as you go: the orchid head, the ribbon, the feather and the Hedera leaves. Cut off the excess wires and tape over; you could also bind on a shaped piece of aluminium wire.

4. Attach the design to the back of the bracelet using ribbon ties; use glue for extra security if required.

5. Check that all the materials are securely fastened, that none is damaged, and that the design is 'faced' into position. Mist and store.

....

Bridesmaid Novelties

'Novelties' is the term given to the designs that will be carried by the bridesmaids at a wedding ceremony. In this part of the book more contemporary designs are shown, but these are subject to fashion and demand, and traditional alternatives are still requested, such as a small basket design with fresh flowers (the size of the basket will depend on the height of the child).

Foliage Bag
MATERIALS
Fresh flowers and foliages
Seven Ruscus hypophyllum
One Mini Cymbidium orchid
One Alstroemeria 'X-treme'
One Eucalyptus parvifolia
Five Ficinea fasicularis (flexi-grass)

Sundries
Half a block of dry foam
Piece of wet foam
Headed pins
Floral spray, pink
90mm wires
Pink paper wires
Pink beaded wire garland

Beaded flower picks

SUITABILITY
This bag is a hand-held design suitable for a bridesmaid from about twelve years of age upwards – an older child in view of the safety factor because of the way the leaves are pinned on. Alternatively it could be placed on a mirrored plate for a dinner party, or as a wedding centrepiece, or as a contemporary corporate design. A host of different-shaped designs can be created by cutting and carving the dry foam.

Storage (florist)
Store the bag in dark, cool area until delivery or collection, and mist according to the materials used. For transportation, put the design in a prepared box with a cellophane cover.

1. Cut the dry foam and add the wet insert.

2. Pin on the base leaves.

3. Pin on the side leaves.

4. Continue pinning on leaves.

5. Attach the handle.

Care (customer)

Avoid placing the design in direct sunlight; keep it cool until you are ready to use it.

METHOD

1. Cut the dry foam into the desired shape; carve a small cavity into the top of the 'bag' and insert wet foam to fit.

2. Pin Ruscus with steel pins into the base of the shape.

3. Butt the leaves up against each other so that the foam is completely concealed; repeat the process at the top of the bag.

4. A nice option is to spray the leaves to match the flower choice. Pin the sprayed leaves onto the foam using headed pins, and pin another row of leaves with the headed pins so as to conceal any steel pins.

5. Make a handle: if the bag is to be carried, ensure that this is both strong and secure – this is achieved by strengthening the handle with paper-covered wires. It is made from five stems of flexi grass with paper-covered wires combined with a beaded garland. Cut it to fit, and pin it on each side with 90mm wires folded over to create hair pins – add blobs of glue to the pinned areas. Once the glue is dry, conceal it with single leaves and pin it on.

6. Add the foliage: Eucalyptus and Ruscus,

6. The finished design.

including a few sprayed leaves to match the bag; insert these into the wet foam, making sure they are not too high – if the bag is to be held, the hand must be able to hold the handle comfortably. Cut and add the Cymbidium orchids, and fill with Alstroemeria. Finish off with beaded picks.

7. Check that the handle is secure, that the materials are securely attached and undamaged, and that none of the foam can be seen. Mist spray as necessary.

ALTERNATIVES TO THE DESIGN
Alternative flowers could be Dendrobium orchid, small Rosa, spray Rosa, Gloriosa. Alternative foliage could be Hedera leaves, or Gaultheria shallon; any other flat leaf would also be suitable. Also the foliage could be sprayed many different colours. A variety of bag shapes can be achieved by carving the dry foam into different shapes; also coloured foam could be used, perhaps partially covered with leaves.

Sisal Bag

MATERIALS
Fresh flowers and foliages
Five Hedera leaves
Sprig of Genista
One Phalaenopsis orchid head

Sundries
Lemon and mint sisal
Gold aluminium wire, decorative gold bullion
Assorted beads
Floristry glue
Wired edged ribbon

SUITABILITY
This novelty bag can be made in varying sizes to suit both the young and the more mature bridesmaid; it might also be carried by the more mature bride, or the bride who wishes for a more contemporary hand-held design, or for a civil service.

Storage (florist)
Store this bag in a dark, cool area until delivery or collection, and mist according to the materials used. To transport, put it in

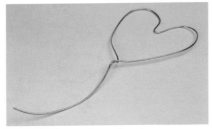

1. Create the outline frame.

2. Attach the wire ribbon handle to the frame.

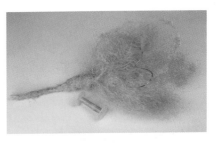

3. Wrap the sisal on to the frame.

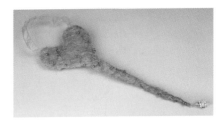

4. The finished sisal shape.

5. Glue on the flowers.

6. The finished design.

a prepared box and cover with cellophane.

Care (customer)

Avoid placing the design in direct sunlight, in draughts, near fruit, or where it will be vulnerable to fluctuating temperatures. Handle it with care before the ceremony.

METHOD

1. Bend the aluminium wire to the desired outline shape – this will form the skeleton on which you will bind on the sisal: be careful not to make it too large, as the finished design will be larger that the original wire frame.

2. Cut out a strip of wired, edged ribbon, long enough to make a handle that can be carried with ease, bearing in mind the size and age of the carrier. Gather the ribbon away from the wire edges so that the wires show about 6cm, then bind the exposed wires of the ribbon tightly on to the aluminium frame, thereby creating the handle.

3. Fluff out the sisal so that it has no solid areas – this makes it more even when you bind it on; the featured design has a blend of two different colours. Next, bind the sisal on to the aluminium frame using appropriately coloured decorative wires and wired garlands – bullion wires work well. Bind on tightly until you achieve your favoured outline shape.

4. A nice option is to add a jewel drop to the end of the design. This part of the novelty could be prepared in advance of the delivery day, as long as it is carefully stored away from direct sunlight and damp conditions.

5. Using floral glue, stick the fresh materials onto the prepared sisal shape.

6. Finally check that all the materials are

secure, that all the wires are finished well and tucked away so there are no obvious loose or sharp edges, and that the handle is secure.

ALTERNATIVE OPTIONS

By using different-coloured sisal, alternative looks can be achieved – though be careful with some colours as they are not all colourfast. Different outline shapes can be made with the flowers, and with geometric and two-dimensional shapes – for these, sandwich two flat shapes together, 'stitching' at the sides with decorative wires.

Any flower chosen should tolerate being out of water, or artificial flowers could be used – in particular this could be a good option if the customer has hay fever. Fresh flower alternatives might be Ornithogalum, Nerine, hyacinth or hydrangea florets, or individual petals.

Pomanders

The pomander or 'flower ball' is a novelty that has never been out of fashion. Over the decades it has taken different forms using a variety of colours and flora, but at the present time it can be either contemporary – suitable for a young adult or for an Asian wedding – or traditional, suitable for a young girl up to the age of nine or ten years old. The meaning of 'pomander' dates back to the early French pomme d'ambre meaning 'apple of amber', and identified as a ball of resin impregnated with herbs and perfumes which was worn or carried; it was thought to protect against disease.

Pomanders are generally spherical, made from either wet or dry foam spheres that are available in a variety of sizes from 8cm. Wet foam has the obvious advantage in that the moisture ensures the materials remain fresh for a longer period; however, soaking the foam can make the pomander quite heavy, and the foam could break if handled incorrectly. A dry foam sphere is

light and will not disintegrate as easily, but it should always be used with dried or silk flowers.

Pomander, Contemporary Style

MATERIALS
Fresh flowers and foliages
Two stems of Cotinus
Three white Rosa 'Akito'
A quarter stem of Gypsophila

Sundries
Beads
Decorative crystal-headed pins
Decorative wire
120mm wires
Floristry tape

SUITABILITY
This is a bridesmaid novelty that is hand held. Traditionally made pomanders are constructed with small flowers and foliages equally spaced throughout the design (similar in construction to the Topiary, see Chapter 7 Function Designs) – and are generally held by younger bridesmaids. However, contemporary finished designs like the one featured here have a more mature feel. Pomanders with multiple spheres may be carried by Asian brides.

Storage (florist)

Store the pomander in a dark, cool area until delivery or collection, and mist according to the materials used.

Care (customer)

Avoid placing the pomander in direct sunlight, in draughts, near fruit, or in fluctuating temperatures. Handle with care before the ceremony.

METHOD

1. Select a sphere of wet foam; contemporary designs with foliage that is bound flat or pinned on need a bigger sized sphere; also the size of the sphere should be appropriate to the

height and size of the carrier. Great care is required when preparing a sphere for use – do not oversoak: not only will this make it heavy to carry, but it could drip, or worse still, the handle could tear through the sphere. A quick dunk into a bucket of water for a maximum of five seconds is enough, or better still, just a generous spray of water.

2. Select materials for the handle: either ribbon to complement the flowers chosen, or beads, which gives the design a sophisticated feel (a necklace could be used for this). Ensure the handle is long enough to carry comfortably; also, do not make it too big for the younger maid as small hands will find it difficult to hold, or it could drag on the floor. Tape two 120mm wires, then bend them over to create a super-large hairpin shape, and thread them through the handle. Pierce all the way through the sphere and pull them down until the handle is flush with the sphere.

3. Cut a selection of Cotinus leaves, of a similar size – this will give an even coverage. Start by placing leaves at the base of the sphere with decorative headed pins, layering one leaf over the other.

4. Continue until the whole sphere is covered. A nice option to finish is to wrap bullion decorative wire over the covered sphere.

5. Insert the gypsophila at the base of the handle, and add three Rosas to finish.

6. To finish off the design, hook the handle wires back into the base of the design by bending and pushing the wires into the sphere. If adding a decorative drop, thread this on to the wire before inserting it (as an alternative to a drop

you could use a curtain tassel).

7. Check that the sphere is completely covered with material, that the handle is secure, and drop finish in place. Carefully spray the design.

ALTERNATIVE IDEAS
Other foliages that could be used are Hedera helix, stripped Aspidistra leaves, Aspidistra 'Milky Way', Scencio leaves, Gaultheria shallon. Leaves can be sprayed many colours. Alternative focal flowers could be Dendrobium orchids, Cymbidium orchids.

5. Add the flowers at the base of the handle.

6. Bend over the wires to fix the handle.

1 & 2. Insert the wires and attach the handle by pushing it right through the sphere.

3. Pin on the leaves.

4. The completed leaf stage.

7. The finished design.

Chapter 7
Function Designs

When creating designs for function décor it is important not only to satisfy your customer with a suitable design, but to be able to transport it safely, or if creating it on site, to be fully prepared with all essential equipment and information for working in that particular site, whether it be a place of worship or a large hotel. A site visit is therefore essential in acquiring information on layout so as to be able to suggest design placements, and to familiarize yourself with the personnel and the location.

The sort of information that you will need is suggested below, and if you cannot obtain it on your site visit, then try a phone call either to a church contact or to the hotel's function manager.

Other weddings: If in a place of worship, are there any other weddings that day – and if there are, would it be possible to liaise with the other bride to share in the costs of flowers so more designs could be provided for both weddings? If this is not possible, when will the other designs be removed?

Entry: Are you permitted entry to the place of worship the evening before to decorate? Get the contact name and number of the key holder to the church – it could be the church warden or the flower ladies.

Access: In a hotel, access to the function room is normally restricted to the day of the function only – so see how early they will allow you to enter, and find out when the tables will be 'clothed up' – it may be

that on request the hotel will cloth up the top table and cake table early.

Water: If you are in a place of worship, where is the source of water? It might be in a kitchen, which may be locked up on the day of the wedding, in which case you will need to bring your foam pre-soaked, with a bottle of water to top it up.

Ladder: If your designs require hanging, will you need a ladder? Is there one you can borrow, and if so, where is it stored?

Pedestals, candlestick holders: It may be possible to borrow church pedestals or candlestick holders in a place of worship, so find out where they are stored, and check that your mechanics will fit on the top.

Lighting: Look at the lighting and natural light to see if certain colours need to be avoided – dark, receding colours will disappear in a poorly lit venue.

Fixing points: In an older building or place of worship, check on fixing points: if there are pew ends, see the best way of fixing designs to them securely and safely. If windowsill designs have been requested, check that the sills are level and deep enough to take a design. Also check the fixing points for overhead hanging designs. Remember that under no circumstances should you insert any of your own fixing points, and treat your surroundings and the interior with the utmost respect.

Site of designs: If decorating in a church or a place of worship, check with the vicar that the positions of the designs are acceptable, and that they allow access to the bridal party, choir, bell ringers and so on.

Disposal of designs: Decide with your customer what should be done with the designs after the function or ceremony.

TOOLS NEEDED FOR OFF-SITE DÉCOR

When working off site you should have a mini version of your toolbox. It must include secateurs, scissors, knife, wires, binding wire, pot tape. You should also have the following:

- Watering can

- Dustpan and brush, with bin bags to dispose of stems and foliage. Be prepared to take away all your rubbish. A useful tip is to work over a flower box: you can work tidily and clear up fast by just putting the lid on and removing the box!

- Towels, to place under any hanging design created in foam that could drip!

- Water mister

- Picnic rug or sheet of plastic: place all buckets on this to avoid marking the flooring. It also helps considerably in clearing up the foliages and stems cut in constructing a design

In addition to the above, ensure that you have a bucket with a few spare foliages and flowers in the event of any damage to materials in transport.

LEFT: Topiary tree.

Measuring up: Take a tape measure to measure design areas, such as windowsills, fireplace mantels, and the length of garlanding required around pillars and doorways.

Be wary of parking at the venues you go to, especially if you are on a tight schedule and need to travel on elsewhere to decorate or deliver other items. It is easy to get blocked in until after the ceremony is over, causing stress and potentially the late delivery of other items. Be aware of any customs when working in a house of worship, and respect the cultures – for example, in a synagogue, male employees will need to cover their head.

If you are well prepared and package all the items carefully, venue decorating is one of the most visually rewarding types of floral design.

Pew Ends

Pew ends are a beautiful wedding or church celebration décor. The design is hung in a variety of different ways, depending on the shape and style of the pew end itself.

A site visit is essential before deciding on the style of the designs and how to fix them on: basically the end shape of the pew holds the key as to how you can attach the design both safely and without damage to the pew end itself.

Pew end designs can be modern – ideal for a newly built place of worship – with limited bold flowers and manipulated foliage, or traditional in their choice of materials and outline shape, enhancing an older, historic place of worship.

Once it has been decided how the design is to be hung, the following factors must also be considered:

Choice of flower/foliage: There should be no thorns or spikes on flowers or foliage, as these could easily catch on the congregation's clothing, or – worse still – the bridal veil. Equally there should be no pollen, and if lilies or flowers with coloured pollen are chosen, then all pollen sacs must be carefully removed so they do not transfer onto clothing as people brush by. And no berries – squashy berries have the same problem, of easily transferring to clothing or the floor of the church.

The outline shape and profile: The design should not extend too much in profile – the pew ends will be sited on opposite sides of the aisle, so the bride and groom must have enough room to walk in between them down the aisle. Similarly the outline shape should enhance the shape of the pew end and should not extend above it, as this would make entrance into the pew awkward for congregation members, and also the flowers would risk being damaged.

The scale of the design: Most pew ends

TIED PEW ENDS	
Advantages	Disadvantages
Natural-looking bouquets	Limited selection of designs
Designs are easily transported to the venue – one bucket can hold quite a few designs; then the stems need drying off and the bows adding	Stems are not in water, which limits the choice of flowers – for instance Lathyrus odoratus (sweet pea) would not hold for the whole day without water
Designs can be made in advance and kept fresh in a bucket of water	Can look old-fashioned
Designs do not drip	

PEW ENDS IN FOAM	
Stems are in water so a larger choice of flowers can be used	Can drip – may need to be hung before installing
It is possible to create a large variety of shapes and designs	Difficult to transport in bulk
Designs can be made in advance	Can be more intricate to construct and therefore more expensive
Designs can be relocated after the ceremony has taken place: eg chair backs for bride and groom, cake table décor; make sure that moisture does not transfer to tablecloths: use suitable mechanics to avoid this	

are not that high, so the size of the finished design is important – it does not want to be trailing on the floor. Also the sides of the design are on view as much as the front, so care must be given to colour and interest in this area.

The number of pew ends: Pew-end designs are sold in pairs, and hung on opposing pew ends, and a variety of options may be suggested to the customer, such as every pew end, every other pew end, or the first few pew ends only.

Two main styles are available – tied or in foam.

Pew End in Foam

MATERIALS
Fresh flowers and foliages
Two Ruscus racemosa (soft ruscus)
Four Arachniodes adiantiforms (leather leaf)
Seven Veronica (secondary flowers)
One Limonium sinuatum 'Blue Star' (statice) (secondary flower)
Three Eustoma 'Charm Picotee Blauw' (focal flowers)
One Gypsophila (filler flower)
Six Liriope muscari (china grass)
Three medium Hedera helix (ivy)

Sundries
Small shovel
Quarter block of wet foam
6mm pot tape
Ribbon, to hang the design

SUITABILITY
Mainly a hanging design intended to hang on a pew end; it could, however, be used for a door, church gate, column or chair back. It could also be used flat to decorate the venue, for example laid flat on a table.

Storage (florist)
Store the design in a dark, cool area until

1. Create the foliage outline.

2. Insert the rest of the foliage.

3. Add the Eustoma and Gypsophila.

4. Add the diagonal placements.

delivery or collection; top up the foam with water as required, and mist according to the materials used.

Care (customer)
As these designs are sited for the customer there are no care instructions.

METHOD

1. Attach the soaked and cut foam with two strips of 6mm pot tape, avoiding the middle of the foam to allow for central placements. The desired outline should be narrow and not too long (an elongated diamond). Start by inserting Ruscus so that it conceals the handle, then double the length of this placement to create the longer length.

2. Add the side foliages: their length should not extend beyond the length of the handle. Angle the foliages downwards so that the sides of the pew end shovel are thoroughly concealed – remember that these will be on view. Insert the rest of the foliages: Ruscus pieces along the focal line, and Arachniodes adiantiforms along the width, creating a nice profile.

3. Add Gypsophila (filler flowers) throughout the design to create visual balance. Next add the focal line of flowers – in this case Eustoma – in an imaginary vertical line, starting with buds and grading up to the largest focal head where the two lines of foliages cross, then grading down again in size to the base of the design.

4. Add a diagonal line of cut Veronicas, then add an opposing diagonal line of Limonium (both secondary flowers).

5. An attractive option is to add plaited china grass in loops down the vertical line to support the focal flowers.

6. Check that all the materials are secure

5. The finished design, with plaited grass added.

and free of damage, and that there is plenty of interest down both sides of the design. Spray if appropriate (note that it is not advisable to spray dark Eustomas because the petals will mark).

ALTERNATIVE DESIGN OPTIONS

Alternatively a tied design could be used (see the next method) for pew ends, or tulle/ organza bows, or simple trails of Hedera helix (ivy) could be hung instead. Pomander-style spheres could be hung on lantern holders. In larger churches where the aisle is wider, topiary-style designs could be used, or small plants with pots wrapped in tulle or organza.

Tied Pew End

MATERIALS
Fresh flowers and foliages
Four Rosa 'Sorbet Avalanche'
Three Alstroemeria 'X-treme'
Three Aspidistra 'Milky Way'
Four Liriope gigantea (lily grass)
Two Eucalyptus cinerea
Five Alchemilla mollis

Sundries
Pot tape and string
Scissors and secateurs
Ribbon, to hang the design

SUITABILITY
A hanging design intended to hang on a pew end. It could also be hung on a door, a church gate, a column or a chair back.

Storage (florist)
Keep the stems in water until the design is ready to deliver and install; once at the venue dry off the stems, add the bow, and mist if appropriate to the materials used.

Care (customer)
These designs are sited for the customer so there are no care instructions.

METHOD

1. The construction technique is the same as the technique for both tied sheaves and flat pack spiralled stems: place the stems that lie on one side diagonally under the binding point; the stems down the centre straight; and the stems that lie on the opposite side, on the

1. Create the outline shape.

2. Start to add the flowers.

opposite diagonal, over the binding point (the binding point is the point where the design is held). The outline shape is a triangle. Start to create the tip of the design using foliage to form a recognizable triangle.

2. Start to add the flowers: the filler flower is the Alchemilla mollis with the Astroemeria on each side of the triangle; the Rosas will form the central focal line.

3. Continue to add the flowers: stagger the Rosas up the central focal line for more

3. Finish inserting the flowers.

4. Tie off the binding point and add the pot tape.

The finished design complete with bow.

pleasing visual interest, layering them with foliage where required, so the beauty of each individual flower can be seen. The final Rosa must be very close to the binding point. An attractive extra touch is to add a couple of loops of grass on each side of the final Rosa.

4. Tie off the design with string and pot tape; on the second binding of the pot tape twist it so that it lies sticky side up – this will help with attaching the ribbon finish. Trim the stems: the length of these will depend on the pew end – too long and they will stand proud.

5. Add the ribbon finish when the design is ready to hang.

6. Check that all the materials are secure and free of damage, and that there is plenty of interest down both sides of the design. Spray if appropriate.

Garlanding

Decorative garlanding dates back to early Roman times – today it is still popular, and is a versatile design for a florist for decorating venues and homes for special occasions.

As with pew ends, fixing the garland is a key consideration. Health and safety needs to be considered when using garlands over entrance doorways, such as a church entrance, or other overhead fixings. A site visit is essential to see whether there are any existing fixing points available for such a hanging design. Measurements for the garlanded area must be taken carefully, as garlanding is normally sold to the customer by the metre.

To calculate the length of garlanding needed, the formulae in the table opposite can be used.

The formulae in the table can also be applied when measuring up garlanding for mantlepieces and stair banisters.

There are three methods of garland construction:

- Using ready-made garland frames – some hook together and are filled with wet foam, other ready-bought garlands are held together by mesh.
- Wiring bundles of assorted foliages onto string or rope (see the Christmas design project in Chapter 9 Seasonal Designs, which is constructed using this method).
- Using trails of foliage such as Hedera or Ruscus racemosa to a thin string or rope, then adding in flowers with plastic phials.

Garland with Ready-made Plastic Frames

MATERIALS
Fresh flowers and foliages
Six cream Eustoma russellianum
Twenty small Rosa 'Aspen'
Four Chrysanthemum spray 'Feeling Green'
Two Nigella
Five Pittosporum tobira
Five Pittosporum tenuifolium
Three good stems of Eucalyptus cinerea

Sundries
Five garland frames
Wet foam (makes 90cm of garland)
Decorative ribbon
Scissors
Fixing wire or string

SUITABILITY

This design is suitable for fireplaces; stair banisters; the top tables at weddings; the registrar's table; the cake table; columns both inside and outside; the entrance to the venue; for church pulpits, and for the function's marquee.

This style of garlanding can be very heavy and takes a lot more fresh flowers to create, therefore making it an expensive design; however, the fresh materials do last because they are in wet foam, and for a summer wedding this requirement could be essential.

After use the garland frames could be reused with fresh wet foam.

If large amounts of garlanding are required, transport could be a problem, and it might be necessary to transport them hanging.

Storage (florist)

Store the garland in a dark, cool area until delivery or collection; mist spray the foam as required. Ensure that the sited garland is secure, and that all the 'mechanics' are hidden from view.

Care (customer)

If this design is sited for the customer there are no special care instructions.

METHOD
1. Soak the foam and hook the frames together.

2. Cut up the foliages and insert them from one end of the foam to the other – start with the larger foliages first. Watch the profile and outline shape.

3. Insert the remainder of the smaller foliages until the foam is completely covered and hidden.

1. Soak the frames and hook them together.

2. Add the large foliages.

3. Complete the foliages.

4. The finished design.

4. Cut and insert the flowers so they create a visual balance. An attractive optional extra is to add decorative bows at each end, securing them with wire.

ALTERNATIVE FLOWERS
When choosing appropriate alternative flowers consider their profile and weight – some would be very unsuitable, for example Tropical heliconia.

Foliage Garlands
MATERIALS
Fresh flowers and foliages
Nine Hedera helix trails
Six small Rosa 'Aspen'

Sundries
Heavy floristry string
Decorative ribbon
Scissors
Plastic phials

32mm-gauge binding wire

SUITABILITY
Refer to the ready-made garland frames above for suggested placements. This style of garland is a cheaper alternative than using ready-made garland frames because it uses less fresh material; nevertheless it is still an attractive design. It also has the advantage to the florist that it can be made in advance, the flowers/ribbon/tulle finish being added once the garland is in situ. It is therefore easy to transport.

Storage (florist)
Store the garland in a dark, cool area until delivery: if constructed from Hedera trails, it can be made a few days in advance. Spray finish the garland thoroughly, and store it in a sealed, dark bin bag. When placed on site, ensure that it is well secured and that all mechanics are hidden from view.

METHOD
1. Cut the string longer than required: the additional length could be used to help fix the garland at the venue; it could also be secured at each end to keep the string taut, which helps when fixing on the Hedera during construction. Using

1. Bind the Hedera trails to the string.

2. The completed foliage garland.

3. Adding the individual Rosa.

binding wire, secure a couple of ends of Hedera trails, and then wrap the Hedera round the string – when at the end of the trail, secure with binding wire.

2. Continue this process until all the string is concealed and covered, and the desired length is achieved. You may need to thicken parts of the garland due to the nature of the Hedera trails, and this can be achieved by binding on additional trails. At this point you can mist the garland and store it in a black bin bag.

3. Using plastic flower phials (orchid phials are ideal for this, as they can be collected and stored from prior deliveries of this product), add water to the phials, cut and insert a focal flower, and then bind it tightly on to the garland – the adding of flowers in this individual manner is best done when the garland is placed in situ, so you can judge accurately the best position for them. Note that you can decorate and conceal the phials if required by wrapping either ribbon or large individual leaves around them (this task can be completed before the function date).

4. Add decorative bows of ribbon, tulle or organza.

5. Complete your quality checks: ensure that all mechanics are hidden, and that all materials are secure.

4. The finished garland.

Cake Decorations

Although fresh flowers are a beautiful adornment to any celebration cake, many considerations must be applied to the choice of flowers and the style of the design. The following are questions that a florist should ask about the cake:

Size: The overall size of the cake or cakes will dictate the size and style of the floral design suggested.

Shape: As above, the outline shape of the cake/cakes will influence the shape of the design.

Tiered: Is the cake tiered, and if so, how many tiers are there? And if the florist is required to make a design to fit in between the tiers, they will need to know the dimension between the tiers.

Finish of the cake: Is the cake iced, and if so, does it have a coloured ribbon or sugar icing flowers? And if decorated with sugar flowers, what type of flower is being represented, and in what colour?

Cake stand: Is the cake displayed on a stand? And if so, what style of stand is it? Could it be decorated?

Staging: Find out if the cake is being professionally staged – but do not get involved in staging the cake, as this is a trained art in itself.

From a floral point of view, having flowers so near food is potentially very hazardous, so careful thought must be given to the toxic properties of the fresh materials. You may have to place greaseproof paper between the design and the cake; or use a silk floral alternative.

There are several designs that are suitable for decorating the top of a cake:

- A small floral vase with a few fresh materials in water: this could definitely

1. Create the outline shape.

2. Add the remainder of the foliage.

3. Add the filler flower.

be the correct choice of design if the flowers required needed plenty of water, for example Lathyrus odoratus (sweet peas).
- Wired posy design: a lightweight design that would be ideal on top of a multi-tiered cake where any additional weight could be an issue. (The construction for this design is similar to a wired posy corsage – see Chapter 6, Wedding Designs.)
- Wired circlet-style design: this lightweight design rests on the cake. (The construction is similar to a wired circlet – see Chapter 6, Wedding Designs.)
- Wet foam for fresh flowers: use a small piece of foam, ideally in a mini deco (a coffee jar lid works equally well as a container) for a posy-style design. A mini table deco is great for a larger square cake.
- Designs that go round the base of the cake: for example a floral wreath ring, or if the cake is displayed on a table it could have garlanding and bows round the table on the cloth.

Cake Design in Foam

MATERIALS
Fresh flowers and foliages
Six medium Hedera leaves (ivy)

4. Insert the Eustoma and Lavandula.

5. The finished design.

One stem of Eucalyptus parvifolia
One Pittosporum tenufolium
One Gypsophila 'My Pink' (filler flower)
Fifteen Lavandula (lavender) (secondary flowers)
One Eustoma 'Adom' (focal flower)

Sundries
One wet mini deco

Ribbon
Assorted wires

SUITABILITY
This design is intended to be placed on top of the celebration cake, for example the wedding cake, the anniversary celebration, retirement or engagement cake, or the cake at a christening or a confirmation.

Storage (florist)
Store the design in a dark, cool area until delivery or collection; top up the foam with water as required, and mist according to the materials used.

METHOD
1. Create a circular outline shape by placing a row of Hedera helix leaves into the base of the mini deco, together with a Eucalyptus, being sure to retain the round outline.

2. Place Eucalyptus and Pittosporum in the foam so as to make a raised profile.

3. Insert Gypsophila throughout the design, again keeping within the foliage profile.

4. Insert the focal flowers Eustoma – one bud high and in the middle, and three smaller heads around this placement. Finish off the focal flowers with the three largest flower heads of Eustoma around the base. Add Lavandula (the secondary flowers) throughout the design.

5. Finish off the design by adding any appropriate accessories, for example beads, wired picks, butterflies, or – as in the photographic option – a couple of ribbon loops to match the cake finish.

6. Check that all the materials are secure, and that the foam is covered; mist the materials as appropriate.

ALTERNATIVE FLOWER/FOLIAGES
Generally, flora choices for cake décor should be small and foliages bushy and compact. Flower alternatives might be spray Rosa, Freesia, Astilbe, Astrantia, Bouvardia, Chamelaucium, spray chrysanthemum, spray Dianthus. For foliage alternatives Hebe, Rosmarinus, Buxus, Myrtus could be used.

The Topiary Tree

Topiary trees are inspired by the formal gardens of old, emulating the clipped box, bay and yew hedges. A variety of stem choices can be used: twisted willow, cinnamon sticks, bamboo sticks, Cornus, and actual tree trunks or bamboo poles for larger designs. This is a great design for decorating functions, and one which has great impact.

MATERIALS
Fresh flowers and foliages
Twelve Rosa 'Cherry Brandy'
Four Hypericum
Four berried Hedera helix (tree ivy)
One Eucalyptus parvifolia
One Rosmarinus officinalis (rosemary)
Piece of Plagiothecium undulatum (flat moss)
Salix stem

Sundries
9cm sphere of wet foam
Two-thirds of a block of wet foam, or size to

1 & 2. Insert the 'stem' into the prepared container and fix on the sphere; measure up the foliages.

3. Add the foliages.

4. Insert the focal flowers – Rosa.

5. Insert the secondary flower – Hypericum.

6. The finished design.

fit the container
Container
Cellophane
Florist's knife and scissors
Secateurs

SUITABILITY

This florist's topiary is a design where the florist creates a mock tree consisting of many foliages and flowers. It has a great range of variety in size and style: it can be small and used as a table décor for assorted functions, or the larger version can be floor-standing and used to embellish the entrance to the church, marquee or hotel. As well as the classic ball shape, the topiary works equally well as a cone shape or a double ball, with the stem showing or no stem showing. An alternative is to make a long-lasting tree with dried plant material. A floor-standing topiary is best made in situ due to its weight, and the difficulty of transporting it. It is a good design to suggest when height but not width is required.

Storage (florist)

Store the topiary in a dark, cool area until delivery or collection; top up the foam with water as required. If delivering a topiary design, ensure that it is firmly secured in the vehicle of transport due to its top-heavy nature.

Care (customer)

If this design is sited for the customer there are no special care instructions.

METHOD

This design is a small-scale topiary suitable for a table top.

1. Choose a suitable container and add some weight to it: for a long-lasting design this can be achieved with sand or pebbles, and for a function design with soaked foam, inserted into a container lined with cellophane. Add a 'stem' for the tree, cut to the appropriate length – if it is intended for a table-top décor ensure that it is long enough not to interfere with the eye line of the guests (you should always be able to see who is sitting opposite).

2. Soak a sphere – though be careful not to oversoak it, as this will result in it being difficult to secure on the 'stem'. Push the sphere on to the 'stem' up to the centre of the sphere. Start to cut your foliages, checking the size: first cut two pieces of foliage the same size and hold them one on each side of the sphere to gauge the diameter – once happy with this, cut a pile of foliages to this size. Start to insert the pre-cut eucalyptus to create an overall ball shape.

3. Cut the secondary foliage, Rosmarinus officinalis (rosemary), and add throughout the design. Cut the berried Hedera (ivy) and insert this, too – the berries help create a good feeling of recession into this design, and provide another contrast of texture with the berried heads.

4. Start to add the Rosa, inserting them so they have a slightly raised profile over the foliage and are spaced evenly throughout the design.

5. Add a secondary flower – in the photographed example Hypericum is used.

6. Finish the design by cutting a piece of flat moss to fit and disguise the foam used in the base of the container (you may need to secure the moss with a couple of hair pins from 71-gauge wire); add a Rosa and a stem of Hypericum to give the finished design harmony.

7. Make your quality checks: ensure that all flowers and foliages are secure in the sphere, and that you have managed to achieve a round shape with no foam showing. Spray thoroughly, due to the fact that the sphere has not been generously soaked.

ALTERNATIVE DESIGNS

Choose small flowers for your focal choice, such as Germini, spray chrysanthemums, spray Dianthus, Eustoma heads, Carthamus. For filler flowers you could use Chamelaucium (wax flower), Gypsophila, Liminonium, and for foliages Pittosporum, Myrtle, Buxus, Aparagus umbellatus – small bushy ones work best.

Topiary trees can be very successful as a long-lasting dried design, where a dry sphere and artificial leaves and flowers are used. Nuts and cones could also be used. Make sure that you add weight to the base of the container – this is even more important if dried materials are being used, since they are very light.

With a floor-standing design the container needs to be a third filled with quick-drying cement, with the mock tree stem inserted into it: this could be a broomstick, a natural branch or a bamboo stick. Secure to the top of the tree stem a couple of wet foam bricks (or a large wet sphere) covered in chicken wire; then repeat the construction method as for the table design.

Raised Buffet Designs

Raised Vase Arrangement

MATERIALS
Fresh flowers and foliages
Five Ruscus hypophyllum
Two Chrysanthemum 'Feeling Green'
(secondary flowers)
Two Eucalyptus parvifolia
Twelve Rosa 'Memory Lane' (focal flowers)
Four Alchemilla mollis (filler flowers)

Sundries
Clear tray (to fit the vase top)
Goldfish bowl vase
Quarter block of wet foam or cylinder
Ten skeletonized leaves
Frog and fix
Coloured water-storing crystals

SUITABILITY
This style of design is used to decorate a buffet table: by keeping the base narrow – in the example photographed this is achieved by the narrow vase base – it leaves more room on the table for the food and drinks to be laid out, without contamination of the foods by the fresh floral materials. The colour of this design makes it suitable for a little girl's christening or a special girl's birthday celebration. Filling the vase with water-storing crystals makes a nice heavy base, which helps its stability if the buffet table is knocked by hungry guests! Buffet designs can have a variety of outline shapes and can be front facing only if the buffet table is sited against a wall; however, there is a general rule that the floral design should not be any more than one and a half times the height of the chosen vase/ container.

Storage (florist)
Store the design in a dark, cool area until delivery or collection. Top up the foam with water as required, and mist according to the materials used.

Care (customer)
If this design is sited for the customer there are no special care instructions. However, if it is taken home after the function, top up the foam with water every couple of days, and avoid direct sunlight, draughts, fresh fruit and fluctuating temperatures. If the customer is collecting the design, put it in a sturdy box with plenty of packaging to prevent it from falling over during transit. The customer should be advised not to leave the design in a car for any prolonged period of time due to the fluctuations in temperature.

METHOD
1. Fill a fishbowl-style vase with coloured water-storing crystals, and slide some coloured skeletonized leaves down the sides (though first check on their colour fastness). Cut the foam to fit a tray, soak, and attach with a frog and fix. Secure the tray with several pieces of fix to the neck of the vase. (Always use a tray that fits the vase and can be secured firmly to it – if it is in the least insecure once the wet foam and the weight of the flowers are added, the arrangement is at risk of falling off the top of the vase.)

2. Insert the Eucalyptus and Ruscus into the foam – the first step is to put a ring of foliage round the base where the tray meets the vase to conceal this area – angle the foliages downwards, then insert them across the foam until it is hidden from view. Create an appropriate outline profile – this vase is round, so a round profile with the foliage has been achieved. Contrast of texture is achieved by combining the shiny Ruscus with the matt Eucalyptus.

3. Add the Rosa – the focal flowers – equally across the design, so that visual balance is achieved. The Rosa must have a slightly higher profile than the foliage.

1. Prepare the vase and the mechanics.

2. Add foliages, creating a round profile.

3. Add in the focal Rosa.

4. The finished design with all the flower material in place.

4. Add the filler flower Alchemilla mollis across the design, and then similarly the secondary flowers Chrysanthemum throughout the design. Cut these materials slightly shorter than the Rosa to create a feeling of recession. Lastly add some rolled, skeletonized leaves to link the interior vase finish to the top design (this creates good harmony).

5. Check that all the materials are secure and free of damage, and that there is interest all the way round the design. Spray the materials if appropriate. Top up the foam with water if required.

ALTERNATIVE DESIGNS
By using different containers and flower choices, a huge variety of designs can be achieved — for example, a traditional flower choice of Dianthus and chrysanthemums in a vase; or more contemporary with bold, tropical flowers and a modern cocktail-shaped vase. Many functions can be catered for with this design, from retirement parties to wedding anniversary celebrations, engagement celebrations, special birthdays, wedding receptions or corporate events.

Candelabra Arrangement
MATERIALS
Fresh flowers and foliages
Eight Matthiola incana 'Carmen' (stock) (focal flowers)
Seven cream Eustoma russellianum (secondary flowers)
Two Panicum (fountain grass)
Eight Sedum (filler flowers)
Two good stems of Eucalyptus cinerea
Nine Hedera helix trails

Sundries
One candelabra
Three pieces of wet foam (cut to fit the candle cups)
Three candle cups
Three candles
Pot tape
Scissors
Secateurs

SUITABILITY
This style of design is used to decorate a buffet table or fireplace mantel: by keeping the base narrow with the use of the candelabra, there is more room on the table for the food and drink to be laid out, without the risk of the fresh floral materials contaminating the food. Buffet designs can have a variety of outline shapes, but can only be front facing if the buffet table is sited against a wall. When incorporating designs that have candles, always check with the venue that candles are permitted.

Storage (florist)
Store the design in a dark, cool area until delivery or collection. Top up the foam with water as required, and mist according to the materials used. Double check on the stability of the candles.

Care (customer)
Ensure the customer is fully briefed on the use of candles — that is, not to leave them unattended, and to be especially careful when children or pets are nearby.

If this design is sited for the customer there are no special care instructions that should be observed during the function; however, if it is taken home after the function it will be necessary to top up the foam with water every couple of days, and to avoid direct sunlight, draughts, fresh fruit and fluctuating temperatures.

If the customer is collecting the design, put it in a sturdy box for the journey, with plenty of packaging to prevent it falling over in transit. Be sure to inform the customer not to leave it in a car for any prolonged period due to fluctuations in temperature.

1. Attach the foam and candle cups securely to the candelabra.

2. Add the foliages, creating the desired outline shape and profile.

3. Add the flowers.

METHOD

1. Attach the candle cups into the candle fittings: if they do not fit snugly, wrap a piece of pot tape round the bottom of each one and try fitting it again. Soak the foam, and using 6mm pot tape, attach it to the candle cup.

2. Insert ivy trails and foliage into the foam so as to achieve the desired outline shape, concealing most of the foam.

3. Next, add in the flowers: use some with a pretty flow quality, such as the Eustoma. Place the scented Matthiola incana (stock) evenly throughout the design. Recess Sedum stems into the design, and finish off with a couple of Panicum (fountain grass) at each end (be careful that wispy materials like this are not placed too near to the candle area).

4. Insert the candles securely into the foam either by using candle holders, or by taping 90mm hairpins to the bottom of the candle (see Chapter 9 Seasonal Designs for guidance). Add some short pieces of foliage to conceal the base of the candles.

5. Finally, check that all the materials are

4. The finished design with the candles in place.

secure and free from damage, and that all the foam is concealed. Spray the materials if appropriate, and top up the foam with water if required.

ALTERNATIVE IDEAS
Different styles of candelabra will need different approaches and material choices. Some candelabras have many candles, and some only one – but always take care that when the candles burn down they will not catch fire to the fresh materials placed round them.

....

Function Table Design

Hurricane Lamp Arrangement

MATERIALS
Fresh flowers and foliages
Three Eucalyptus cinerea
Four Pittosporum tobira
Five Phlox 'Miss Fiona' (filler flowers)
Five Alchemilla mollis (filler flowers)
Eight Matthiola incana (stock) 'Figaro Lavender' (secondary flowers)
Five Paeonia 'Sarah Bernahardt' (focal flowers)
Eight Papaver (poppies) (focal flowers)
Five Ageratum (filler flowers)

Sundries
Wreath ring
Glass hurricane lamp
Floral organza-headed decorative pins
Candle
Floral knife
Scissors

SUITABILITY
This style of design is popular for weddings or other functions where an arrangement is required to sit on a table where people are having a sit-down meal, and it is viewed all the way round. Its real advantage is that it does not interfere with the eye line of customers. The featured

1. Attach the ruched organza edging.

2. Insert the foliages.

3. Add the filler flowers.

4. Add the larger focal flowers.

design is more suitable for a round table such as a dinner party table, or a low coffee table; it could also be used for outdoor functions. The addition of a candle is an attractive option.

Storage (florist)

Store the design in a dark, cool area until delivery or collection. Top up the foam with water as required, and mist according to the materials used.

Care (customer)

If this design is sited for the customer there are no special care instructions that need be observed during the function. However, if it is taken home after the function, they should top up the foam with water every couple of days, and avoid direct sunlight, draughts, fresh fruit and fluctuating temperatures. If the customer is collecting the design, put it in a sturdy box with plenty of packaging to prevent it falling over in transit. Be sure to inform the customer not to leave it in their car for any prolonged period due to fluctuations in temperature. Also advise them on the health and safety issues of using candles.

METHOD

1. Bevel the edges of the foam; soak it with water. To create a luxurious edge, floral organza can be used, securing it with headed pins in a ruched manner on both the inner and outer edges (the

5. Place the hurricane lamp and candle in the wreath ring.

advantage of edging in this way is if many designs are to be made they can be edged up in advance before soaking the foam). Alternatively you can just use foliage.

2. Cut and insert the mixed foliages, layering them in and using many different textures to create maximum visual contrast. When layering the stems into the foam, use a slight angle and clockwise direction (see the design Loose open wreath in Chapter 8 Funeral Designs for guidance.)

3. Add in the filler flowers Alchemilla mollis and the Phlox, creating an equal visual balance with them. Keep the length of these flowers the same as the foliage.

4. Cut and insert the focal flowers, the Paeonia and large-headed Papaver (poppies), placing them evenly round the frame so their profile is slightly higher than the foliages.

5. Once at the venue, place the hurricane lamp in the middle of the wreath ring and place the candle in it, ensuring that it is a snug fit and not wobbly; add a little floral fix to the base of the candlestick for extra security.

6. Check that all the materials are secure and free from damage, and that all the foam is concealed. Spray the materials if appropriate. Top up the foam with water if required.

ALTERNATIVE DESIGNS

Designs can be given seasonal appeal with an appropriate choice of flowers (see Chapter 9 Seasonal Designs for the Christmas version), or themed for special occasions, such as a wedding or special wedding anniversary with the use of colour and/or accessories.

Taking a Funeral Order

It can be a traumatic experience taking a funeral order from an emotional customer or family. Be patient, take the time to listen, and give them time and empathy. Guide them through the selection of tributes available, taking into consideration that this could be the first time they have ordered a funeral tribute – so your gentle advice on what to order is essential.

Do not be embarrassed to discuss money; the family could be disappointed if their tribute appears too small, but it is important to explain the costs of a more complicated design. Also, when faced with an emotional customer, it is easy to agree to a design that you cannot make: better to choose an alternative than have to ring the family back later saying the design will not work. Try and encourage them to personalize the tribute – this could be in the use of a favourite colour or flowers, or reflecting the job or hobby of the deceased.

If you have already taken the same order for the same funeral, advise the customer of this: it will avoid duplication, and therefore offending perhaps close relatives.

Ensure that you obtain all the essential information:

- The full name of the deceased – double check spellings, because mis-spelt names cause unnecessary distress to the family.
- The day and date of the funeral – grieving relatives can get confused at this sad time.
- The time of the funeral.
- The name of the undertaker – this will be your contact to double check the above details, and the time and date of delivery of your funeral tribute. This could differ from the actual day of the funeral.
- The delivery address of tributes – this could be to the family home or to the undertaker.
- The name and contact details of the person placing the order.

Tribute Cards

Writing a tribute card can be an upsetting task for a customer, so it is advisable to provide a selection of cards – the family may wish to take them away and write them in private. On return of the card/s, match the card to the tribute (if there is more than one ordered), and write on the back of the tribute card the name of the deceased in full, as 'T/L Mr/Mrs': the message on the front of the tribute card may not have any direct mention of the name in full, but simply 'Wife', 'Father', or a nickname. Also write down the date and time of the funeral, and it is good practice to add your own contact/company name should the funeral director have a query once the design is delivered.

Then place the tribute card in a cellophane sleeve and attach it securely to the design, either by inserting the card and tape to a specially designed plastic pick, or make a loop over the top with 90mm floristry wire, and secure to the back of the tribute card with clear tape.

Sending a tribute is the last gesture the customer will make for the deceased, so it is essential that no mistakes are made. A well made, well thought through design will help soften the sorrow at the funeral itself.

Choosing a Funeral Design

The Medium

In addition to tied sheaf designs and spray trays with wet foam bricks, there is a massive range of wet foam base shapes to choose from; these include two-dimensional wreath rings, crosses, hearts, open hearts, cushions, pillows, posy pads and letters, and each shape comes in a variety of sizes (with the exception of lettering). There are also novelty shapes that are as diverse as caravans, fish, teddy bears, bottles of beer, to name but a few. As your skill and experience improve there is also a range of three-dimensional shapes: rabbits, teddy bears, gates of heaven – or even cut and style your own

Assorted funeral frames.

LEFT: Loose open posy design.

from wet foam designer sheets. Fashion and trends change and so do the ranges provided by the manufacturers.

General Guidance

There are certain other points to remember when constructing funeral designs. First, designs are not only viewed from above, but also from eye level if they are placed on top of the coffin, so careful attention is needed when placing the edging to ensure that none of the base mechanics can be seen.

Consult with the undertaker on whether any other designs are being placed on top of the coffin – careful negotiation is called for if estranged family members all want to order a five-foot coffin spray each for the same coffin! Furthermore, clearance between the top of the coffin and the inside of the hearse roof could be limited – in the UK it could be as little as 25cm (10in).

Edging

'Edging' is the term given to the treatment of the outer edge of the design: it creates a border in which the fresh materials are inserted. As a general rule, loose open designs have foliage edges, while based designs have ribbon edges – although the customer can choose either. Care needs to be taken in that whatever medium is chosen, the design retains its recognizable outline edge, for example a heart.

Foliage edging: The foam is soaked before the edging is attached, and then the foliage is inserted in various ways. This can be as single leaves, which might be either pinned or inserted; good examples are Hedera helix, Gaultheria shallon or Galax.

Alternatively flat foliage might be used, such as Chamaecyparis (cupressus) or Arachniodes (leather leaf); or massed small foliage – Pittosporum, Asparagus umbellatus – or mixed foliages.

Ribbon edging: In this style of edging the foam is not soaked until the ribbon pleats are pinned on. The pleated ribbon should be neat and regular, and the scale of the pleats dictated by the size of the tribute – thus a posy pad for a small child's coffin would need to be smaller than that for a full size adult's coffin.

Pleats are normally formed by using polypropylene ribbon which is cheap, waterproof and available in a variety of

1. Funeral edging – Gaultheria leaves pinned on.

2. Funeral edging – Cupressus.

3. Funeral edging – mixed foliages.

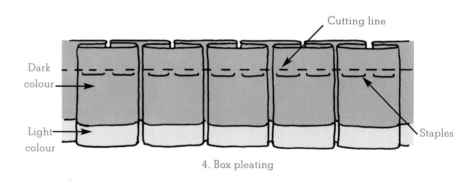

4. Box pleating

5. Funeral edging – double box ribbon edging.

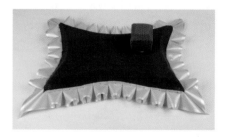

6. Funeral edging – double box pleating with mitred corners.

colours, although trends change and new products become available – jute and pressed sisal ribbon now offer a more contemporary feel (see Loose Open Posy Pad, below). Ribbon pleats are created with a staple and then pinned on to the frame.

There are two main styles of pleating: flat pleating (knife pleating), where the ribbon is overlapped, and box pleating (see diagram); double box pleating looks very formal and neat, and can be created using one or more colours – this is ideal if you are trying to represent a country flag or a favourite football team. (Be careful to put the dark colour over the top of the lighter one if creating double pleating for white chrysanthemum-based designs – failure to do so will result in distortion of the outline shape, especially for lettering.)

Alternative edging: Edging can also be created with moss, bark or organza (floral colourfast), to name but a few. These can be either glued or pinned on.

Funeral and Flower Etiquette across the Religions

Funeral traditions vary for each culture and faith. Here are some general guidelines to help, but if in doubt, check with the local religious leader or the family members.

Christian/Roman Catholic/Protestant:
For all these religions flowers are welcome, both at funeral and memorial services. A huge variety of designs can be sent either direct to the funeral directors or to the house where the funeral cortège leaves from. Flowers for the coffin top are generally from the immediate family only.

Buddhist: Buddhism believes in reincarnation, and sees death as a transition to the next incarnation. Buddhist funerals are therefore a celebration marking the soul's ascent from the body. Flowers may be sent to the family.

Hindu: A Hindu funeral is normally held within twenty-four hours of the death. Friends can call in on the family house where the body is held until the traditional cremation. Visitors may bring flowers, which are placed at the feet of the deceased. An Aum can be used as a traditional symbol of Hinduism.

Jewish: A Jewish funeral service is conducted in a funeral home or the family home as soon as possible after death – normally within twenty-four hours. Only family members attend the burial. Floral tributes are inappropriate at the funeral or during the seven days of mourning, known as the Shivah.

Muslim: This religion buries the deceased as soon as possible, as it is believed that burial is required to free the soul from the body. The Muslim period of mourning is three days; floral tributes are inappropriate.

Sikh: Death is viewed as a separation of the soul, and to be God's will. Cremation is the norm with this religion, and the ashes are either scattered in water or in a place of sentimental value. Floral tributes are acceptable; the Khanda symbol can be used.

Green Funeral: People who are concerned about the effects on the environment that a traditional burial or cremation may have may ask for a burial method more suited to their beliefs. They can choose to be buried in an all-natural bio-degradable green burial shroud, sometimes a simple coffin made of cardboard, or some other bio-degradable material such as wicker. They may choose to be buried in an eco-cemetery, and have a tree planted over their grave as a contribution to the environment and a gesture of remembrance. Floral tributes must therefore be bio-degradable.

Loose Open Style Designs

'Loose open design', or an 'informal' design, is a term that explains the construction of the funeral piece. Generally there are two or more types of flower, which can be in one or more colours. The foliage materials are arranged freely, although some can have a directional property – for instance, they might all be placed in a clockwise direction (see Loose Open Wreath). The focal flowers are support wired (to protect them from damage – see Wiring Techniques in Chapter 6), and are inserted to reinforce the outline shape – for example in a circle for a wreath ring or posy pad.

SUITABILITY
These designs have an informal feel to them; they are suited to both genders and all ages, and are generally ordered by friends, acquaintances, neighbours and distant relatives – although there is no reason why close family members shouldn't order them too, maybe with more expensive flowers or if on a tight budget. Tradition dictates that close family members order a more formal design, such as based tributes (see later in this chapter), but this is not irrefutable, and much depends on individual preference and budget.

Storage (florist)
Store the design in a dark, cool area until it is time for delivery or collection. Top up the foam with water as required, and mist according to the materials used. Ensure before delivery or collection that the tribute card is firmly attached.

Care (customer)
If the customer is collecting the design to take it to the funeral themselves they should be advised about storage and transportation – in particular to avoid any prolonged periods in a car due to the fluctuating temperatures.

Double-Ended Spray

MATERIALS
Fresh flowers and foliages
Five Cocculus
Four Lilium 'Ercolano' (focal flowers)
Eight Pittosporum tobira
Six Ruscus
Twenty Amaranthus
Fifteen Eupatorium (filler flowers)
Eight Leucadendron

Sundries
A three-quarter block of wet foam
Florist's knife, scissors and secateurs
12mm pot tape

SUITABILITY
As above. If the design is made to a large size it would be suitable for placement on the coffin top.

Storage
As above.

METHOD

1. Soak and tape the three-quarter block of wet foam securely onto the tray (as the design is only required to stay fresh for a limited time, a three-quarter block can be used; larger designs will need a full block, or can be made with a double tray, or with specialist coffin-top foam frame). To create the diamond shape, first determine the longest length – this size can be chosen according to the budget, the type of flowers or the final placement, such as the coffin top. Once the longest length has been decided, cut another and insert one at each end of the tray – now visually half the measurement – this becomes the measurement of either side. Cut the Cocculus accordingly, and put all these four pieces firmly into the foam, angling them downwards so that they touch the table.

2. Infill with foliage thereby joining up the four pieces to create the outline shape. (Put the design on to the floor to check that you have achieved this.)

3. Start to add the cut Cocculus into the foam, creating a raised profile – think of an opening fan when placing the Cocculus, working from the base up and then over the top and back to the base. Add the additional foliages – in the photographed example this is Ruscus and Pittosporum. The variegated leaves help to create contrast amongst the foliages.

4. Insert the focal flowers, the lilies, along an imaginary middle horizontal line, with the largest head in the middle – this must also have the most profile in height, with the buds or smallest heads at either end. Then place the transitional sized/medium flowers, staggering these on each side of the horizontal line, depending how many focal flowers are being used.

5. Next add the Amaranthus flowers in two diagonal lines, right to the edges and across the middle focal flowers, but making sure that no flowers extend over the outline shape.

1. Creating the proportions of the outline shape.

2. The outline shape completed.

3. Add the foliages throughout.

4. Add the focal line of Lilium.

5. Add the diagonal placements of Amaranthus.

6. Add the Leucadendron across the middle width.

7. Add the filler flowers.

8. The finished design.

6. Insert the Leucadendron stems across the middle of the design.

7. Cut and insert the filler flowers, making them lower than the main flowers.

8. Finally check that the outline shape is still clearly visible, that all the materials are firm, that all the foam is concealed, and that no materials are damaged. Insert the tribute card.

ALTERNATIVE FLOWERS
For focal flower use Dianthus, Gerberas, Chrysanthemum blooms, Helianthus (sunflowers), Rosa, Paeonia.

For filler flowers, Alchemilla mollis (in summer) Anigozanthus, Astilbe (in summer) Bupleurum, Limonium, Solidago trachelium.

Single-Ended Spray
The outline shape of this design resembles a tear drop, so has a symbolic representation.

MATERIALS
Fresh flowers and foliages
Four Eucalyptus cinerea
Four Ruscus hypophyllum
Six Tulipa 'Golden Parade'
Five Gerbera 'Dino'
Eight Achillea 'Parker's Variety'
Five Phlox 'Miss Fiona'
Six Delphinium 'Sydney Purple'
Three good stems Cupressus

Sundries
Tray
A half block of foam
Pot tape
71mm-gauge floral tape
Florist's knife, scissors, secateurs

SUITABILITY
As above.

1. Preparing the outline.

2. Creating the proportions of the outline shape.

4. Add the Cupressus throughout.

Storage
As above.

METHOD
1. Soak the foam. Place the half block of foam into an oblong container, securing it with two strips of 12mm pot tape. (Just half a block may be used for this style of design to save money, without compromising its purpose, but if a larger scale design is required, then use

3. The outline shape completed.

5. Add the contrast foliage.

6. Support wire the Gerberas.

7. Add the focal flowers.

8. Add the diagonal placements.

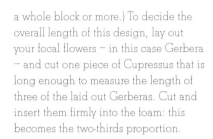

a whole block or more.) To decide the overall length of this design, lay out your focal flowers – in this case Gerbera – and cut one piece of Cupressus that is long enough to measure the length of three of the laid out Gerberas. Cut and insert them firmly into the foam: this becomes the two-thirds proportion.

2. Now cut three pieces of Cupressus: these will become one third of the length. This is worked out by measuring from the middle of the foam to the tip of the inserted Cupressus; then halve this measurement, and cut the three pieces of Cupressus to this determined length. Defoliate them and insert them firmly: this forms the outline skeleton on which to create the outline teardrop.

3. Add the cut Cupressus into the base of the foam, continuing to fill in the outline shape; you could lay the design on the floor to check the shape.

9. Add the filler flowers throughout, and the Tulipa across the width to finish the design.

4. Add the Cupressus throughout the design, radiating the foliage from the focal area, just off centre.

5. To add contrast to the foliage base, add a line of Eucalyptus cinerea from long length to long length; add Ruscus hypophyllum, optional across the width.

6. Support wire the Gerberas, using the cup and saucer method: this support method allows you to angle the finished Gerberas so that they face upwards. Tape a 70mm wire and hold the end on to the calyx. Holding onto the end of the taped wire with your thumb, twist the wire round the calyx, and then spiral down the stem. The aim is to tightly support the calyx.

7. Add the Gerbera as shown. The flowers at each end should be smaller (if possible), and the focal Gerbera the largest with the tallest profile. These three flowers are on an imaginary centre line; the other two placements should be staggered each side of it. Ensure that all the Gerberas are evenly spaced.

8. Create a diagonal line of Delphinium from top right to bottom left, making sure that the colour goes to the edge of the foliage, but does not extend outside it. The foliage acts as a protector in addition to creating the outline shape. Create an opposite diagonal line of Phlox from top left to bottom right.

9. Finish off the design with a row of Tulipa across the width, and Achillea recessed down the focal line.

10. Check that the outline shape is still clearly visible, that all the materials are firm and all the foam is concealed, and that no materials are damaged. Store in the dark because the Tulipa are very phototrophic (they grow to the light). Insert the tribute card firmly.

ALTERNATIVE FLOWERS
Alternative focal flowers could be Dianthus, Gerberas, Chrysanthemum blooms, Helianthus (sunflowers), Rosa, Paeonia.

For filler flowers you could use Alchemilla mollis (summer), Anigozanthus, Astilbe (summer), Bupleurum, Limonium, Solidago Trachelium.

Single-Ended Spray with Stems

This arrangement is a twist on a tied sheaf design because the mock stems are placed in foam; this has the advantage that you can build the profile angling each head into the desired position, which is almost impossible to achieve if the stems are tied together and are able to take up moisture.

MATERIALS
Fresh flowers and foliages
One Cupressus
Two stems of Eucalyptus parvifolia
Three stems of Pittosporum tenufolium
Fifteen Dianthus 'Prado' (focal flower)
Ten white Veronica caya
Six Dianthus 'Green Tick'
Two spray Chrysanthemum
Three Aspidistra leaves

Sundries
Two-thirds of a block of wet foam
Pot tape
One long tray
Florist's knife and scissors

SUITABILITY
As above.

Storage
As above

METHOD
1. Secure the part-block of soaked wet foam to one end of the tray using 12mm pot tape.

2. Create an outline of Cupressus: once

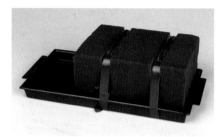
1. Attach the foam to the tray.

2. Create the outline shape.

3. Add the foliage throughout.

4. Add the focal flowers.

5. The diagonal placement of
chrysanthemums and Veronica.

6. The folded Aspidistra leaves
making the bow.

7. The 'pretend' stems added to finish the design.

you have determined the longest length
and inserted it into the foam, create the
width by cutting a piece of Cupressus
that fits into the longest length twice
(this becomes a third of the overall
design, see Single-Ended Spray above
for guidance). After you have inserted
these three pieces, fill in the outline
shape to create a triangle.

3. Cut the Cupressus and insert it into the

foam to create a full profile – add the
cut Eucalyptus pieces and Pittosporum
throughout to add contrast to the
foliaged shape. Position the foliage so
that it radiates in profile from the
bottom centre.

4. Support wire the Dianthus – the focal
flowers – using the external method (see
Wiring Techniques at the beginning of
Chapter 6), and insert them, staggering

them down the centre of the design.
Use the Dianthus that are in bud along
the outside edges to help create a good
rhythm.

5. Add a diagonal line of chrysanthemums
from the bottom right to the top left.
Then add a line of Veronica across the
opposing diagonal, from top right to
bottom left.

6. Fold over an Aspidistra leaf – this will become one side of the 'bow'. Repeat this on a second leaf and insert it into the end of the design.

7. Add some mock stems, using the leftover stems from making the design: use a mixture to create a true 'pretend' sheaf. Ensure that some of them are as long as one of the widths (to create a third): this will help to achieve a realistic-looking spray. Finish the stems off by cutting them to a shape, and not straight across; be careful not to cut them too short otherwise they will look out of proportion. (These must be firmly inserted as some people may pick up the design by the stems, unaware that they are 'pretend'.) To create a feeling of recession, add six stems of Dianthus 'Tick' low into the design.

8. Finally check that all the foam is covered, that all the materials are secure, and that there is no damaged material. Spray, and make sure the tribute card is firmly inserted.

ALTERNATIVE IDEAS
Other focal flower choice could be Gerberas, Rosa or Helianthus (sunflowers). By using tropical foliage – say, palm instead of Cupressus, and Anthurium instead of Dianthus – this design could take a very modern approach.

Loose Open-style Wreath Ring

The symbol of the wreath denotes the eternal circle of life: it dates back to the ancient Greeks and Romans as a symbol at funerals, and is still a very popular choice of funeral design.

MATERIALS
Fresh flowers and foliages
Two Cupressus
Three Arachniodes adiantiformis
Six Rosa (focal flower)
Six Rosa 'Viva' (secondary focal flower)
Ten Narcissus 'Grand Soleil d'Or' (secondary flower)
Eight Iris 'Blue Magic' (secondary flower)
Five Tulipa 'Parade'
Two Acacia (mimosa) (filler flower)

1. Making the foliage edging.

2. Create a herringbone pattern with the different foliages.

3. The foliaged design.

4. The design with the filler flowers added.

5. With the focal Rosa added.

6. Inserting the secondary flowers.

Sundries
12in wreath ring
Florist's wires
Florist's knife and scissors
Secateurs

SUITABILITY
As above.

Storage
As above.

METHOD

1. Bevel both the inside and the outside edges of the wreath ring. Soak the frame. Cut the Cupressus into similar lengths and create a foliage edge, angling the foliage downwards so that it touches the table and creates movement either clockwise or anticlockwise. Continue this process until all the outer and inner edges have been completed.

2. Add the foliages Eucalyptus, Arachniodes and Cupressus into the top and sides of the wreath, working a herringbone pattern on the top.

3. Continue 'greening up' the foam with the foliage, until it is completely covered.

4. Cut and add in the Acacia (mimosa – the filler flower) throughout the design until a nice balance has been achieved.

5. Support wire the Rosa using the external support wire method (see Wiring Techniques at the beginning of Chapter 6). Cut the large-headed Rosa so that when they are placed into the foam they are a little proud of the foliage. First, lay them onto the wreath ring to be sure they are equally spaced and make a regular pattern; then insert them firmly into the foam.

6. Repeat the support wire method for the smaller Rosa 'Viva' (yellow in colour); cut them slightly shorter than the larger-headed rose so that when they are inserted into foam they are slighter lower and therefore recessed. Insert the Narcissus on the inner and outer edges: note that the stems of these spring flowers are soft and can be difficult to insert into foam without shattering them – if this happens, pre-make a little hole using a tougher stem and then insert the soft stem into this pre-made hole.

7. Add the final secondary flowers, the Iris and Tulipa, around the outer and inner wreath ring.

8. Finally, make your quality checks: ensure that all the foam is covered, and that all the materials are secure and that none is damaged. Spray with water, and check that the tribute card is firmly attached.

ALTERNATIVE CHOICES
The photographed example contains a very seasonal choice of spring flowers, but the same design could be made to reflect the other seasons using appropriate flowers. Thus for summer, the focal flower could be Peony or Helianthus (sunflower), for autumn Dahlia, and for winter Erynigum. You could use different foliage for the foliage edge – for example ivy leaves, Galax leaves, Pittosporum or Arachniodes adiantiformis, or create a mixed foliage edge. Alternatively a ribbon edge could be substituted for the foliage edge.

7. The finished design.

Loose Open-Style Posy Pad

The colours in this particular tribute would suit a man or a woman, and the jute overlay ribbon and apples give this traditional design a modern twist, making it suitable for a wider range of ages. The apples could be a link to the deceased, perhaps a favourite fruit, or maybe they had their own apple orchard.

MATERIALS
Fresh flowers and foliages
Four Arachniodes adiantiformis
Two Eucalyptus 'Parvifolia'
Five Rosa 'Passion' (focal flower)
Three Chrysanthemum 'Feeling Green'
Five Malus large (apple) (for focal interest)
Eight Malus small (crab apples)
Four Hypericum 'Envy Flair' (filler flower)
Three Alchemilla mollis (filler flower)

Sundries
12in posy pad
Florist's knife and scissors

Stapler
Staples
Ribbon: polyribbon and jute ribbon
70gsm wires
Wooden picks
12mm pot tape
Steel pins

SUITABILITY
As above.

Storage
As above.

METHOD
1. Using two ribbons, staple together a box-pleated ribbon length that will fit all the way round the posy pad. This design uses a jute red ribbon over lime, colours that will complement the chosen flowers. Cut off the excess hem. Bevel the edges of the posy pad to a 45-

1. Prepare the box pleating.

2. Pin on the pleating.

3. The completed pleating.

4. Add the foliages.

5. The completed foliages.

6. Measuring the Rosa.

7. Insert the Rosa.

8. Insert the Malus.

9. The finished design.

degree angle, and stick 12mm pot tape round the join of the polyfoam and foam base.

2. Pin each individual pleat onto the frame, angling the pin down through the ribbon, pot tape and into the polyfoam base.

3. Continue to pin on the ribbon, all the way round the posy pad. Soak the frame.

4. Cut the Arachniodes adiantiformis into small pieces and put these into the foam – put them in at an acute angle so as to cover the foam and create a circular movement, but being careful not to cover too much of the ribbon edging.

5. Cut the Eucalyptus into small pieces and add these into the design, mingling them with the Arachniodes adiantiformis, and again giving the design movement.

6. Support wire the Rosa (the focal flowers), using the external method (see Wiring Techniques at the beginning of Chapter 6 for guidance). Prepare the Malus (apples) for the design by inserting wooden picks into the base of each one. Next, lay out the wired Rosa on to the posy so they are spaced out evenly.

7. Then insert the Rosa into the foam, keeping the stems vertical and checking again on the spacing. The easiest way to check that the Rosa are evenly spaced

is to put the design on the floor.

8. Next put the prepared Malus (apples) into the design, again ensuring that they are equally spaced and that the wooden picks are vertical. Cut the Malus so they are a little lower than the roses, to help create a feeling of recession.

9. Add the remaining filler materials – Chrysanthemum, Hypericum, Alchemilla mollis and baby Malus – into the design: these should be firmly inserted at the same angle to give the same directional movement as the foliage, and creating an even distribution of colour and texture.

10. Check that all the foam is covered, that all the pins for the ribbon edge are concealed, and that all materials are secure and none are damaged. Spray the design, and make sure the tribute card is firmly inserted.

ALTERNATIVE IDEAS
This classic funeral tribute lends itself to many design variations: a foliage edge could be used instead of ribbon edging, for example Cupressus, Galax leaves, Pittosporum; or use different focal flowers – Gerberas or Germinis, Open Lilium flower heads, Chrysanthemum blooms. Posy pad frames are available in a large selection of sizes, too.

Loose Open-Style Heart

The heart is a symbol of love and tenderness – this informal design would be suitable to order for a close relative, such as an auntie or a close friend, or even a much loved community member, for example a teacher or a lollipop lady.

MATERIALS
Fresh flowers and foliages
Five Rosa 'Ilos'

1. Prepare the heart frame.

2. Attaching the ribbon edge.

3. Pin down the centre of the heart.

4. Mitre the corner – step one.

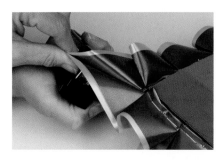

5. Mitre the corner – step two.

6. Add the foliages.

7. Add the filler flowers.

8. Add the focal flowers and the headed pins.

Three Solidaster
Two Santini (chrysanthemums)
Three Eryngium
One Cupressus
Two Arachniodes adiantiformis

Sundries
Six blue-headed pins
12in heart frame
Ribbon
Pot tape
Stapler, staples
Florist's knife, scissors and secateurs

SUITABILITY
As above.

Storage
As above

METHOD

1. Bevel the edges of the heart shape to a 45-degree angle to the polyfoam base. To improve the top bevelling around the 'lobes', cut down the centre. Stick pot tape all the way round the shape so that half of it sticks to the foam, and half to the polyfoam – this will give extra security to the ribbon edging.

2. Prepare two lengths of double ribbon box pleating, choosing the colours carefully – this is the cheapest part of the sundry selection but it has a significant impact on the overall colour influence. Ensure that each length fits from the bottom point of the heart around the edge to the middle cleavage, plus 4in (this is approximately three to four pleats); then cut off the hem with the exception of the ribbon – this will create the middle cleavage, the last three to four pleats. Start pinning the ribbon to the design, using one pin for each pleat, starting from the bottom point and working your way round the heart shape.

3. Once at the middle of the heart, pin the ribbon pleats down the cleavage using the hem that you did not cut off for extra security – you may find it useful to use long mossing pins for extra anchorage. When you pin the cleavage area, ensure that the ribbon pleats 'match' so they mirror each other.

4. Staple the bottom point, creating a mitre join – line up the two colours, then lift up the ribbon and staple as near as you can to the frame.

5. Then lower the ribbon and staple together, keeping the ribbons lined up and following the centre line so that it continues the heart point. Soak the foam.

6. Add the foliages to each half of the heart, so that they follow its shape: this gives movement to the design (be careful not to cover the ribbon edging).

7. Add the Santini and Solidaster into the foam using the same angle and movement as the foliage – ensure equal distribution of colour so as to create visual balance.

8. Support wire the roses with the external method using 70gsm wires. Add the wired focal roses in a regular pattern, so they are equally spaced and in an upright position. Insert the Eryngium heads so they are lower than the roses, and upright: their lower position, together with the colour, will give a feeling of recession to the design. An optional distinctive touch would be to add a blue-headed pin to each of the Eryngium heads.

9. Check that all the oasis is covered, and all the materials secure. Mist the flowers and insert the tribute card.

Loose Open-Style Cross

With its obvious religious links, this informal design is particularly suitable for someone with strong Christian belief/connections; it offers bereaved

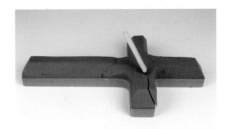

1. Prepare the cross frame.

2. Prepare the box pleating.

3. Attach the box pleating.

4. Mitre the corner, step one.

5. Mitre the corner, step two.

families comfort in their time of deep sorrow.

MATERIALS
Fresh flowers and foliages
Six Chrysanthemum

9. Creating contrast with the foliage.

Five Rosa 'Akito'
Four spray white Dianthus
Four Hypericum 'Green Envy'
One Pittosporum tenuifolum
Three Arachniodes adiantiformis
Three Ficinea fascicularis (flexigrass)
One Cupressus

Sundries
12in cross frame
Florist's knife and scissors
Stapler and staples
Polyribbon and sisal ribbon
70mm wires
12mm pot tape
Steel pins

6. Trim the excess ribbon.

10. Position the focal Chrysanthemum.

11. Inserting the secondary flowers.

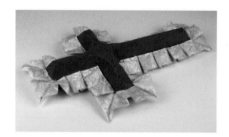
7. The completed ribbon edge.

8. Covering the foam with the foliage.

12. Adding optional features.

SUITABILITY
As above.

Storage
As above.

METHOD
1. Bevel the edges at a 45-degree angle. Stick 12mm pot tape all the way round the frame, and across the seam of the frame where the polyfoam and foam meets.

2. Prepare double ribbon edging for a 12in cross. For this size cross you will need to prepare the following strips: four single pleats – the width of the pleat must not exceed the width of the frame – four x two pleats for the 'cross bar', two x three pleats for the tip of the cross, and two x five pleats for the long bar – leave additional ribbon lengths on each side to make the mitred corners later. This recipe will differ for larger frames – the trick in preparation is to keep the pleats on each side equal due to the symmetric property of the shape.

3. Start to pin on the pleats, starting with the single pleats: put two pins into each pleat, angling the pin into and through the ribbon, the pot tape and into the polyfoam base.

4. Pin on all the other strips of box-pleated ribbon, using one pin per pleat. Start to create the mitred corners. Fold the ribbon of each strip inwards so they face each other, then pull them up and staple them as near to the frame as possible.

5. Then pull the ribbon corner down, ensuring that the angle is an extension of the foam frame and staple.

6. Trim off the excess ribbon, and continue this process until all the corners are neatly and evenly finished.

7. To complete the inner corners of the ribbon, just trim flush to the frame. Then soak the frame.

8. Cut up the Cupressus and Arachniodes into small lengths; place into the foam at an acute angle, starting at the ends of the foam and working to the middle of the cross: this creates a feeling of movement, as all the materials radiate from the centre. Carry on with this process until all the foam has a basic covering.

9. Add the Pittosporum: a variegated leaf, this adds contrast to the design.

10. Support wire the Chrysanthemum using the external method. Cut them to the same size so their heads stand proud of the foliage, and insert the stems vertically; space them evenly into the design.

11. Cut five small Rosa to the same length so their heads are shorter than the Chrysanthemum – this creates a feeling of recession. Cut the Dianthus into small pieces and add them throughout the design – this extends the colour to the edges.

12. An optional distinctive feature is to thread Hypericum berries onto flexi grass and add this to the frame (see Leaf manipulation). Another option is to make 'leaves' out of the sisal ribbon and insert them round the central Chrysanthemum.

13. Check that all the foam is covered, that all the pins for the ribbon edge are covered, and that all the materials are secure and none is damaged. Spray the design, and make sure that the tribute card is firmly inserted.

ALTERNATIVE IDEAS
This is a classic funeral design – often one large cross is used as a single design on the coffin top. You could use a foliage edge such as Cupressus, ivy leaves, Pittosporum or Asparagus umbellatus instead of ribbon edging; and different focal flowers – Gerberas or Germinis, Open Lilium flower heads, Rosa.

....

Sympathy Basket

MATERIALS
Fresh flowers and foliages
Five Helianthus annuus 'Sunrich orange' (sunflower), focal flower
Two Amaranthus
Three Alchemilla mollis
Two Chrysanthemum 'Feeling Green'
Four Achillea 'Parker's Variety'
Four spray Dianthus
Two Ruscus hypophyllum
Four Cotinus
Three Hedera helix (ivy) trails
One-eighth bunch of Gaultheria Shallon

Sundries
One block of foam
One trug-style basket
Cellophane
Secateurs
Florist's knife and scissors

SUITABILITY
This trug-style sympathy basket is an informal design suitable for a person who loved flowers and the countryside. It is suitable for a man or a woman, depending on the choice of colour. The traditional, country-style choice of flowers works well in this style of basket, making it more suitable for a middle-aged person. In addition to these considerations this design could be 'recycled' and given to a hospice or care home; flowers at a cremation are often there for only a short time before being removed, so a tribute can be used elsewhere, or if a customer is struggling to justify the cost of the flowers. A nice twist to this design is to green up

1. Line the basket and secure the foam.

2. Add the foliages.

3. Add the focal flowers and the flowers down the central line.

4. Add the remainder of the flowers.

5. Profile of the finished design.

6. The finished design.

the trug and then give it to the family for the younger members to pick their own flowers and add into it – maybe from their grandparents' garden if it is for one of the grandparents.

Storage
As above.

Customer care
As above.

METHOD
1. Line the trug basket with cellophane, and cut the foam so that it stands proud of the rim – tuck in the excess cellophane so that the foam is secure (if the foam is a snug fit securing with pot tape may not be necessary).

2. Create a length outline with soft Ruscus, ensuring that you have the same length

protruding at each end of the trug. Insert a line of hard Ruscus across the basket, so the foliage radiates out from under the handle in the middle. The last line of foliage is the Gaultheria shallon across the width of the basket (from one side to the other).

3. Add a line of focal flowers, Helianthus annus (sunflower) – if the floral choice allows, put smaller heads at each end, with the largest flower upright under the handle (but so you can still put your hand to hold the handle). Place other focal line flowers on either side of the main focal flower: imagine a central line, then put a flower at each end and one on the centre of this line, and two flowers just to each side of the focal flowers. Reinforce the focal line with trails of ivy and Amaranthus.

4. The remaining flowers and foliages will introduce a feeling of recession into the design: Cotinus, Chrysanthemum, Alchemilla mollis, Achillea and spray Dianthus.

5. Ensure that all the materials are secure and free of damage, and that there is no foam showing. Then mist the design, and insert the tribute card.

ALTERNATIVE FLOWER CHOICE
This design is best created with garden-style flowers.
Focal alternatives: Paeonia, Dahlia, Chrysanthemum bloom.
Filler alternatives: Aster, Astilbe, Phlox, Sweet William.
Secondary flower alternatives: Matthiola, Delphinium – Larkspur.

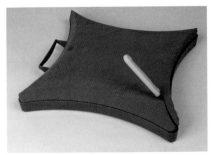

1. Prepare the frame.

2. Pin the leaves on the corners.

3. The outside foliage layer.

4. Add the next layer of leaves with the reverse side uppermost.

5. Insert the flowers.

6. Continue to cover the foam with materials of different texture.

Textured Pillow

MATERIALS
Fresh flowers and foliages
Two Anthurium 'Midori'
One Gerbera 'Dino'
Five Achillea 'Parker's variety'
Two Hypericum 'Green Condor'
One Chrysanthemum 'Feeling Green'
One yellow spray Dianthus
One Amaranthus
One Aspidistra
One third of a bunch of Gaultheria shallon

Sundries
33 × 33cm (13 × 13in) cushion
Decorative pins
Dressmaking pins
Florist's knife and scissors

SUITABILITY
This contemporary informal design is
suitable for a trendy young man or woman.
Visually its effectiveness depends on the

7. The finished design.

contrast of textures – smooth textures next to rough, shiny next to matt – and the balance of bold colours.

Storage
Store at room temperature due to the inclusion of Anthurium – these damage if they are kept too cold.

Customer care
As before.

METHOD
1. Bevel the edges of a foam cushion to a 45-degree angle; then soak.

2. Cut a selection of Gaultheria shallon leaves; pin three on each corner, as shown in the photograph.

3. Pin a row of leaves along the edge, making sure that the frame edge is concealed; pin with dressmaker or mossing pins.

4. Pin the next layer of leaves with the reverse side uppermost: this gives a great contrast. Pin them so that they overlap on to the first row of leaves, on the outside edge with dressmaker pins and the tips with coloured-headed pins.

5. Cover the rest of the foam: place a couple of strips of cut Aspidistra leaves flat on to the frame, and attach them with decorative-headed pins – this shiny surface creates a great contrast with the matt underside of the Gaultheria leaves. Next add Amaranthus using small hairpins of floristry wire– this fluffy surface also makes a good visual contrast to the Gaultheria leaves. Insert an Anthurium head – this creates not only a little height but also an umbrella effect with its waxy surface over the fluffy Amaranthus and matt Gaultheria leaves.

6. Continue to cover the foam with

materials of different texture: the shiny Hypericum berries next to the matt petals of the Dianthus and the grainy texture of the Achillea. Be sure to create a visual balance of colour with the green and dominant primary colour of the yellow.

7. Check that the outline shape is still clearly visible, that all the materials are firm and none is damaged, and that all the foam is concealed. Insert the tribute card.

ALTERNATIVE IDEAS
This concept of handling textured materials can be applied to most foam shapes including a heart, pillow, cross or wreath. When choosing materials, look at the visual textures and select those that achieve maximum visual contrast (see Chapter 3 Elements and Principles for ideas on texture choices).

....

Tied Funeral Designs

Tied Sheaf

MATERIALS
Fresh flowers and foliages
Seven Rosa 'Avalanche Peach'
Ten Amaranthus
Eight Eupatorium
Eight Pittosporum tobira
Five Leucadendron 'Kameleon'
Four Brassica 'White Crane'
Two Anthurium leaves
Four copper beech leaves
Four Ruscus
Seven Cocculus leaves

Sundries
Polyribbon
Assorted wires
Pot tape and string
Florist's knife and scissors
Secateurs

Tribute card

SUITABILITY
A classic, informal funeral tribute: the tied sheaf – the name derives from a sheaf of corn – offers a traditional or modern style depending on the choice of flower and

1. Create the outline shape.

2. Add the focal materials down the central line.

3. Add the side placements, spiralling the stems.

4. Add the lower side placements.

5. Tie off the design.

6. Add the tribute card and pot tape.

7. The finished design.

foliage, from classic Lilium to tropical flowers. It is a great design to offer for a green funeral, needing no gift wrap (ensure no coated wires are used to support the wire or the polyribbon to finish), and for a last minute request (often on the way to the funeral). It is suitable for young or old, man or woman. The design caters for different budgets, too.

This design is not suitable to be taken apart after the funeral as a lot of the stems will be too short for a vase; if this is a requirement of the customer, suggest more of a flat pack version (see Chapter 4 Tied Designs).

Storage (florist)

Store the sheaf upright in a bucket of water in a dark, cool area until delivery or collection, when the stems will need to be dried off.

METHOD

1. The construction of a sheaf requires strong pieces of backing foliage evenly balanced on each side of a straight central stem – this creates a triangle outline. Use the same spiralling technique as for flat pack construction (see Chapter 4), so that all the stems angled to the right of the design pass underneath the binding point and the stems angled to the left, over the binding point. Prepare the stems as for tied work by removing all foliage below the binding point. In this design use the stems of Cocculus to create the desired shape.

2. To create maximum visual interest, add some copper beech leaves within the shape. Next put in the central placements, layering Rosa, Eupatorium and foliages: these stems go straight down the middle.

3. The next step is to add materials on each side, to create interesting lines: use Brassica layered with foliages angled to

the right, slipping all stems under the binding point. The Lecadendron is placed with layered foliages on the left, with stems over the binding point.

4. To create a bottom line, add Amaranthus on each side (still using the under and over spiralling technique); to finish the bottom of the triangular shape, add an Anthurium leaf on each side.

5. Continue to layer materials until you have reached the binding point – the central rose will have the most profile. Tie off firmly with string.

6. Prepare the tribute card: place the card into a cellophane sleeve, secure it with tape, and then tape it on to the back of a 90mm-gauge wire. Slip one end of the wire under the string, and bend the wire over the string; then secure the card by taping a 12mm pot tape over the tying point – then tie it around again, but twisting it over so that it is sticky side up.

7. Make a double bow, then fix the bow over the binding point – the bow will stick onto the tape to conceal the pot tape; tie the central ribbon above and below the bow. Cut the stems to half the length of the flowers above the binding point. Shape the stems as shown, with a tapering outline.

8. Check that all the stems are secure within the binding point, that no mechanics of the binding point are on show, and that the tribute card is secure. Mist according to the materials used.

....

Based Styles

Based styles are often referred to as 'formal design'. A based design is where most of the chosen frame shape – the heart, or

cushion – is covered with the same material, which is bonded together in order to completely obscure the frame. In the UK market, the white double chrysanthemum is hugely popular to create this style of design. There is, however, a range of other flowers/foliages that could be used in the basing method: coloured Chrysanthemums, for example 'Feeling Green' Dianthus (split the calyx to open it up to maximum size and lower the profile), Eryngium, Gypsophila, Hydrangea heads, Molucella, Rosa, Trachelium, Aspidistra, laurel leaves, blue pine, reindeer moss, flat moss (plagiothecium undulatum). Other materials could be used, as long as they can create tight bonding that covers the frame shapes and keeps the profiles correct for purpose.

Most formal based designs have a small spray of assorted flowers, which should not measure more than a third of the overall surface area, and – if the size of frame allows – a single flower where the tribute card is inserted. Often the single flower is linked to the spray via grasses, for

Based design, using chrysanthemums.

example Xerophyllum tenax (bear grass), ficinea (flexigrass) or ribbon. (Note that this separate placement is optional; it is not always appropriate on a small design where it would look crowded.)

Suitability

Based or formal designs are generally sent to close family members and partners, of either gender, young or old.

Storage (florist)

Based designs should be stored in a dark, cool area until delivery or collection. Top up the foam with water as required, and mist according to the materials used. Ensure before delivery or collection that the tribute card is firmly attached.

Care (customer)

If the customer is collecting the based design to take to the funeral themselves, they should be advised as to storage and transportation – in particular to avoid any prolonged period in a car due to the fluctuating temperatures inside it.

Preparation for Basing Using Chrysanthemums

For most based designs the following basic procedure is applied to prepare the chrysanthemums and insert the heads. Cut and grade to size the chrysanthemum heads to small, medium and large. Cut the stem lengths: small 2.5–4cm (1–1.5in), medium and large heads 4–5cm (1.5–2in).

GENERAL BASING METHODS
Use the small heads to create the first outer layer: the centre of the chrysanthemums, or 'eye', must all face out the same way – try facing them to look at your tummy, if you are standing. Bond the flowers close, but not too close, so that they overlap. Place a row around the whole circumference of the shape. Use the medium heads to create the next layer – these 'eyes' need to 'look' at your face. Try to blend this layer so that it does not create a fringe over the lower layer.

The top layer is created using the larger heads – these 'eyes' face upright. Bond them together but without overlapping or fringing over the inner or outer layer. You may have to pluck a couple of petals off here and there to create a smooth finish.

Number of Chrysanthemum Heads:

Depending on the time of year, you will need to be aware that although each chrysanthemum spray stem will carry many heads, some will be smaller than others and the stems not as strong. Ask your local wholesaler for guidance on stem count if you are not sure.

Based Style Designs

Based-Style Wreath Ring

The symbol of the wreath denotes the eternal circle of life; it dates back to the ancient Greeks and Romans as a symbol at funerals and is still a very popular choice of funeral design.

MATERIALS
Fresh flowers and foliages
Two stems Eucalyptus 'Parvifolia'
One stem Arachniodes adiantiformis
Six stems peach Rosa (focal flower)
One Limonium 'Maine Blue' (filler flower)
Twelve stems double Chrysanthemum (basing flower)
Four Veronica 'Pacific Ocean' (secondary focal)
Six Ficinea fascicularis (flexigrass)

Sundries
12in wet foam wreath ring
Small piece of wet foam for bump
70mm wires
Tribute card and pick
12mm pot tape
Polyribbon, staples and pins
Florist's knife and scissors

SUITABILITY
As above.

Storage

As above.

METHOD
1. Bevel the outside edge and slightly bevel the inside edge of the wreath ring. Attach a small piece of wet foam to form a bump: do not cut it to the same width as the wreath ring because when the basing is inserted it will distort the outline shape. The correct height is about 1.5cm (0.5in) higher than the basing: to check this, cut a large basing head and insert it temporarily. Attach the bump using 6mm pot tape in two

Graded Chrysanthemums – small, medium and large.

tram lines.

2. Make a strip of box pleating (or edging of your choice – if fresh, you will need to soak the frame) to fit round the circumference of the outer circle; stick 12mm pot tape round the 'join' where the polyfoam and wet foam meet. Tear off the excess hem if using double colours. Always use the darkest colour uppermost – lighter colours on the higher side of ribboning of based designs can blend into the flowers and distort the outer shape. Pin on the prepared ribbon using one pin per pleat, angling the pin through the pot tape into the polyfoam. Next, pin coloured polyribbon flat to the inside of the wreath ring, pinning into the polyfoam base. (On a larger wreath ring a strip of box pleating would be used for the inner circle.)

3. Continue this process right round the ring. Do not finish on half a pleat: when you have nearly completed the ribbon attachment, check whether it will fit neatly, and if it doesn't, undo the stapling and make two smaller pleats to fit, or one larger one. Soak the frame.

4. Cut the Chrysanthemum heads and grade them into small, medium and large in size. Cut the stem lengths: small 2.5–4cm (1–1.5in), medium and large heads 4–5cm (1.5–2in) (see Preparation for Basing, above). Use the small heads to create the first layer, with

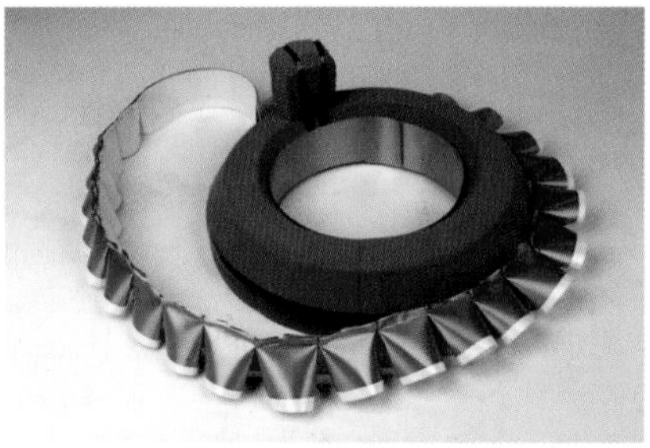

2. Attach the ribbon to the wreath frame.

3. The ribbon attached.

4. The first row of chrysanthemums.

5. The second row of chrysanthemums.

6. The inner row of chrysanthemums.

7. The top row of chrysanthemums.

8. Spray foliage.

9. Flowers in spray.

10. The finished design, with the flexigrass link detail and tribute card flower in place.

third to two thirds using Eucalyptus, and across the width with Arachniodes adiantiformis (this is similar to the single-ended spray, but curved).

9. Add the filler flower – Limonium throughout – recessing it low into the design. Support wire the focal Rosas using the external wiring technique and appropriate weight wire (*see* Wiring Techniques at the beginning of Chapter 6). Insert them in a staggered line – they should be slightly higher than the foliage, with the focal Rosa the highest. Add the Veronicas (the secondary focal flowers) across the diagonals, recessing these by inserting them lower.

10. Add the tribute card Rosa – remove the top basing flower to avoid damaging it. Insert the link material – in this design flexigrass – from the individual flower to the spray, then replace the top basing flower.

11. Complete your routine quality checks: ensure that all the Chrysanthemum heads are bonded smoothly and without fringing, that they are secure, and that no foam is showing. Check that the bump and the fresh materials are all secure and undamaged. Mist the materials. Insert the tribute card near the single Rosa.

ALTERNATIVES TO THE DESIGN
As an alternative, the foam could be based in a different basing material, as discussed earlier in the chapter. Polyribbon edging of different colours might be used, or a different edging altogether, such as foliage. Different flowers, or flowers of a different colour could be used in the spray – for example mini orchids, Eustoma, spray chrysanthemums.

the centre of each Chrysanthemum or 'eye' facing out the same way (at your tummy, if you are standing). Bond the flowers close so that they overlap, but without looking crowded; place a row round the whole circumference.

5. Use the medium heads to make the next layer – these eyes need to 'look' at your face. Try to blend this layer so that it does not create a fringe over the lower layer.

6. Use more medium heads to make an inner concentric circle, making sure that they cover the join between the ribbon

and the foam – face them all at the same angle, so they are closely bonded but not overlapping.

7. The top layer is created using the larger heads – these eyes face upright. Bond them together but without them overlapping or fringing over the inner or outer layer; you may have to pluck off a couple of petals here and there to create a smooth finish.

8. Insert the foliages to create the spray – make a curved design, being careful that it does not extend outside the edge of the frame. Use the proportions one

1. Attach the bump to the frame.

2. Add the foliage edging.

3. The first row of Chrysanthemums.

4. The second row of Chrysanthemums.

5. The top row of Chrysanthemums.

6. The foliage outline of the spray.

7. The completed foliage in the spray.

8. The finished design.

Based-Style Posy Pad

MATERIALS
Fresh flowers and foliages
Eight Rosa 'Blizzard' (focal flower)
A three-quarter bunch of Pittosporum tenufolium
One Arachniodes adiantiformis
One Hypericum 'Green Envy'
Four Muscari liriope (China grass)
One Eucalyptus parvifolia
Twelve Chrysanthemum

Sundries
10in posy pad
Piece of wet foam (for the bump)
Pot tape
90mm-gauge wires
Florist's knife and scissors
Secateurs

SUITABILITY
As above.

Storage
As above.

METHOD
1. Bevel the foam edge, and attach the bump for the spray. In this design the bump is placed in the centre of the foam, but it can be placed off centre – though be careful not to place it too near the edge or the spray will look unbalanced. Cut the foam to fit – to check the height, cut one large chrysanthemum head and insert it into the foam temporarily next to the bump. Stick a line of 12mm pot tape around the base of the bump; pin it into the foam using 90mm wire hairpins, being careful not to cut the pins too long or too short: too long and they will go through the bottom of the posy pad, too short and the bump will not be secure. Soak the frame. Alternatively you can use a 'le bump' fitting – a pre-made bump with a screw attachment (see the next project, the based heart). On a larger posy pad frame the bump can be off centre with a single flower for the tribute card.

2. Cut and insert the Pittosporum tenufolium, angling it downwards so that it obscures the polyfoam at the base of the frame, and is long enough to show once the first row of chrysanthemums is inserted.

3. Grade the chrysanthemums (see Preparation for Basing, above). Use the small heads to create the first layer, placing them so that the centre or 'eye' of each chrysanthemum faces out the same way (angle them to face your tummy). Insert the heads so that they conceal the join of the foliages, bonding them so that they overlap but without looking crowded; place a row round the whole circumference.

4. Use the medium heads to create the next layer – these eyes need to 'look' at your face. Try to blend this layer so that it does not make a fringe over the lower layer. Note that these flowers do not sit on the frame. Continue with this row right round the whole frame.

5. Use the larger heads for the top layer – these 'eyes' face upright. Continue to insert these heads until the whole frame is covered, but leaving the bump still showing.

6. Insert a circle of Arachniodes adiantiformis into the bump to form the circle outline shape of the spray.

7. Next, cut and insert the foliages to create a raised profile.

8. Support wire the Rosa using the external wiring method (see Wiring Techniques at the beginning of Chapter 6). Insert them so as to have one in the centre, three round the focal flower, and three lower on the outer circle.

9. Check that all the chrysanthemum heads are bonded smoothly and without fringing, that they are secure, and that no foam is showing. Check that the bump and the fresh materials are all secure and undamaged. Mist the materials. Insert the tribute card.

ALTERNATIVE DESIGN IDEAS
As an alternative, the design could be edged in different foliages – for example Galax leaves, Hedera helix leaves, Asparagus umbellatus, Arachniodes adiantiformis. Or it could be edged in ribbon in a variety of colours that could either match the flowers or represent a country – for example red/white/blue for France – or a favourite football club.

Based-Style Heart

This emotive heart design would be sent to a very close family member or a dear friend, or even a much loved community member, for example a teacher, or a lollipop lady.

MATERIALS
Fresh flowers and foliages
Twelve Chrysanthemum (basing flower)
Six pale pink Rosa (focal flower)
Two Eucalyptus 'Baby Blue'
Two Astilbe 'Europa' (filler flower)
Small piece of Pittosporum tenufolium
Six Liriope muscari (link grass)

Sundries
12in heart
Mini 'le bump'
Antique pink organza
Decorative headed pins
Assorted wires
Florist's knife and scissors

SUITABILITY
As above.

Storage
As above.

1. Prepare the frame and attach the organza.

2. Screw in 'le bump'.

3. The edging preparation complete.

4. The point of the heart.

5. The first row of chrysanthemums.

6. The second row of chrysanthemums.

7. The top layer of chrysanthemums.

8. The foliage spray.

METHOD

1. Bevel the edges of the heart shape to a 45-degree angle to the polyfoam base. To improve the top bevelling round the 'lobes', cut down the centre (see Loose Open Heart above, for guidance). Start to pin the organza into the polyfoam in the frame using headed pins.

2. Screw in the mini 'le bump', on which you will fashion your spray at a later stage; alternatively a piece of wet foam could be used for a bump – see project instructions for the based posy pad.

3. Soak the frame, and check that the outline shape of the heart has not been obscured by the organza.

4. Cut and grade in size the chrysanthemum heads as before. Use the small heads to create the first layer, starting at the bottom tip of the heart shape, with one head in the centre and two similar-sized heads on either side, thereby creating the point of the heart.

5. Continue with the small heads, making sure that the centre, or 'eye', of each chrysanthemum faces out the same way – try angling them at your tummy, as in the preceding projects. Insert the heads so that they conceal the join of the organza and the foam frame. Bond the flowers so that they overlap but don't look too crowded; place a row round the whole circumference, including the centre cleavage of the heart – keep these eyes looking into the organza, as this will help you achieve a rounded shape around the lobes.

6. Use the medium heads for the next layer, inserting them so that these eyes 'look' at your face; continue thus all the way round the circumference of the heart, as this will help achieve the rounded shape. Down the centre of the

heart face the heads into the organza, and try to blend this layer so that it doesn't create a fringe over the first layer.

7. For the top layer use the larger heads with the eyes facing upright; insert these heads until the whole frame is covered, with just the bump showing.

8. Add the foliages into the spray using the proportions one-third to two-thirds, using the Eucalyptus to create a curved base, into which the flowers will be added later. Recess the Pittosporum into the bump across its width. Make sure that the finished foliage spray does not exceed a third of the overall finished based design.

9. Support wire the Rosa, using the external wiring method. Insert the filler flower, Astilbe, into the prepared foliage spray, then insert the Rosas in a staggered line using the small heads at each end, and the largest head at the point where the two foliages cross. Add a couple of gathered organza Rosas to the spray to make a link with the edging. Remove one of the top based chrysanthemums to insert the individual tribute card flower. Link the spray to the individual flower using the Liriope muscari (china grass).

10. Complete your quality checks: ensure that all the chrysanthemum heads are bonded smoothly and without fringing, that they are secure, and that no foam is showing. Check the bump, and that all the fresh materials are secure and undamaged. Mist the materials, if appropriate, and insert the tribute card.

9. The finished design.

ALTERNATIVE DESIGN IDEAS
As the preceding projects.

1. Prepare the base and measure the height of the Chrysanthemums.

2. Add the Phormium leaves to the edges.

6. The top row of Chrysanthemums completed.

3. Add the Chrysanthemums to the tips of the cross.

7. The foliage added to the spray.

4. Add the first row of Chrysanthemums.

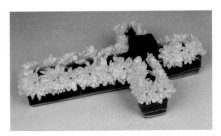

5. The finished first row of Chrysanthemums.

8. The flowers added to the spray.

The finished design with optional leaf links.

Based-Style Cross

With its obvious religious links, this formal design is particularly suitable for someone with strong Christian beliefs and/or connections, offering bereaved families comfort in their time of deep sorrow. It would be suitable for any age, young or old, and any gender.

MATERIALS
Fresh flowers and foliages
Six Rosa 'Sphinx'
One Ruscus racemosa
One Chrysanthemum 'Feeling Green'
Two Alchemilla mollis
One Arachniodes adiantiformis
Nine Chrysanthemum 'Zembla Cream'
Eight Phormium tenax

Sundries
One 12in cross frame
Decorative headed pins
Small piece of foam (for the bump)
Florist's knife and scissors

SUITABILITY
As above.

Storage
As above.

METHOD
1. Attach the bump with a couple of strips of 6mm pot tape. It should stand proud by 2.5cm (1in), and to check that it is the right height, cut one large-headed chrysanthemum and insert it temporarily into the frame. Then soak the frame.

2. Use decorative pins to secure Phormium in strips along the edges of the foam; when going round the corners, fold the leaf to get a sharp edge.

3. Cut and grade the Chrysanthemum as before. Starting at the tips of the foam, insert three small heads at a 45-degree angle so they do not extend over the width – this will help keep the shape of the corners crisp.

4. Insert a row of medium-headed Chrysanthemums all round the outer edge, bonding them closely to each other but without overlapping. As before, the centre 'eyes' of these chrysanthemums should 'look' into your face.

5. Continue this process until the first row of Chrysanthemums is completed.

6. Add the top row, centre eyes of these Chrysanthemums 'face upwards to the sky'. Bond them closely together.

7. Add the foliage to the bump, using the proportions one third to two thirds when cutting and inserting the Ruscus lengthways, and one third either side of Arachniodes adiantiformis (leather leaf). Add the foliages until the foam bump is nearly concealed and the profile is raised at the centre (think of it as a mini single-ended spray). Add the filler flower Alchemilla throughout.

8. Support wire all the Rosa using the external method (see Wiring Techniques at the beginning of Chapter 6 for guidance). Push the Rosas firmly into the bump in a staggered line as shown. Insert a couple of Chrysanthemum 'Feeling Green', recessed on each side. Add the single Rosa to take the tribute card, with a small piece of matching foliage.

9. For the finishing touch – strip down the Phormium tenax into narrow strips and insert around the base of the focal Rosa; pin into the foam as shown.

10. Complete your quality checks: ensure that all the Chrysanthemum heads are bonded smoothly and without fringing, that they are secure, and that no foam is showing. Check that the bump and all the fresh materials are secure and undamaged. Mist the materials. Insert the tribute card.

ALTERNATIVE DESIGN IDEAS
As the preceding projects.

Based Style Pillow

This pillow is a formal design that is suitable for either gender and across all age groups. It would be sent to a close family member or very close friend. The symbolism for using pillows or cushions is to rest your head and sleep for eternity.

MATERIALS
Fresh flowers and foliages
Sixteen double Chrysanthemum basing
One green mini Cymbidium (focal flower)
One Eucalyptus 'Parvifolia'

Two stems of assorted Cape green (filler flower)
One Arachniodes adiantiformis
Nine strands of Xerophyllum tenax

Sundries
14in wet foam pillow
Polyribbon
Assorted wires
12mm pot tape
Staples/pins
Florist's knife and scissors

SUITABILITY
As above.

Storage
As above.

METHOD
1. Bevel the outside edge of the pillow frame. Stick 12mm pot tape round the 'join' where the polyfoam and wet foam meet. Attach a small piece of wet foam for the bump that will take the spray. To check that the bump is the right height, cut one large-headed Chrysanthemum and insert it temporarily into the frame: your bump should be about 2.5cm (1in) higher than the Chrysanthemum. To attach the bump to the frame, attach a

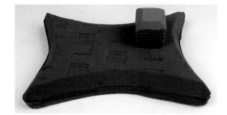
1. Preparing the base.

2. The ribbon edging attached.

3. The first row of Chrysanthemums.

4. The second row of Chrysanthemums.

5. The top row of Chrysanthemums.

6. The foliage added to the spray.

7. The finished design with the plaited grass link.

them together but without them overlapping or fringing over the outer layers. Keep the top layer in rows across to continue the symmetric shape of the foam; you may have to pluck a couple of outer petals off here and there to create a smooth finish.

6. Insert the foliages to create the spray, laying them out in the proportions one third to two thirds, using the Eucalyptus for the longer two-thirds length, and the Arachniodes adiantiformis for the one third, across the width (again, think of a mini curved single-ended spray).

7. Add in the filler flower Cape greens. Support wire the mini Cymbidium orchids – the focal flowers – using the external wiring method (see Wiring Techniques in Chapter 6), and place them in a staggered line the length of the spray. Insert the individual flower for the tribute card, first removing the basing flower that is next to the spray flower to ensure that it does not damage it. Add the link grass – in this design it is plaited Xerophyllum tenax – from the individual flower to the spray.

8. Complete your quality checks: ensure that all the Chrysanthemum heads are bonded smoothly and without fringing, that they are secure, and that no foam is showing. Check the bump, and that all the fresh materials are secure and undamaged. Mist the materials, and finally insert the tribute card.

ALTERNATIVE DESIGN IDEAS
You could base the foam in a different basing material, as discussed earlier in the chapter, or use different colours of polyribbon edging, or different edging, such as foliage. Try using different flowers, or colours of flowers, in the spray – Rosa, Eustoma, spray Chrysanthemums, spray Dianthus.

piece of 12mm pot tape around the base of the bump and pin it to frame using 90mm hairpins (or use a pre-made 'le bump').

2. Make four strips of box pleating to fit the frame, keeping to an equal number of pleats for each side (or add an edging of your choice – for fresh foliage edging you will need to soak frame). Tear off the excess hem if using double colours. Always use the darkest colour on the upper side of the pleats – lighter colours can blend into flowers and distort the outer shape. Using one pin per pleat, pin on the prepared ribbon, angling the pin through the pot tape into the polyfoam. Mitre the ribbon corners (see the technique described in the Loose Open Cross design). Soak the frame.

3. Cut and grade the Chrysanthemums as

before. Use the small heads to make the first layer: starting at the corners, put one head into the foam, then two similar sized heads on either side to create a point. As before, the centre, or 'eye', of each Chrysanthemum must face out the same way – try facing them at your tummy. Bond the flowers so that they overlap but without looking crowded; place a row round the whole circumference of the frame.

4. Use the medium heads to create the next layer – these eyes need to 'look' at your face. Again, start at the corners so that these corner placements continue the bevelled look at the four corners. Blend this layer, being careful that it does not make a fringe over the lower layer.

5. Use the larger heads for the top layer, with the 'eyes' facing upright; bond

Letters

Letters are used to create a personalized tribute, and can be bought individually or as a set of letters – for example NAN, MUM and DAD. The foam letters are available in two options: as a hard plastic base with moulded clips, or a hard foam base with screw-in clips. These letters clip onto a plastic stand that holds the letters upright. The plastic stands are available in different lengths to allow for different length words, as two, three, five and seven letters long, and can be angled so they hold the letters upright or at a slight angle. They are available with extensions and centre supports.

The letters are placed against the side of the coffin inside the hearse, making the tribute highly visible.

Buying the letters individually has the advantage of being able to spell out individual Christian names, nicknames or different language spellings – however, the letters will need to be carefully placed on the bars so the spacing looks right and the word reads easily. Pre-made spelled out words are already attached to the bar so are spaced correctly.

Take care not to oversoak letters, as this can compromise the stability of the bar (for seven letters long, especially) and make it very heavy and awkward to transport, both for the florist and the undertaker.

Based-Style Letters

MATERIALS
Fresh flowers and foliages
Eight stems of Chrysanthemum (depending on variety)
Three Rosa 'Sphinx'
Half a stem of Ruscus racemosa
Half an Arachniodes adiantiformis
One stem Solidaster
Part stem Limonium

Sundries
Foam 'P'
Small piece of foam

Pot tape
Polyribbon, pressed sisal ribbon
Headed decorative pins
Florist's knife and scissors

SUITABILITY
As above.

Storage
As above.

METHOD

1. Attach the bump to the frame; to check the height of the foam bump, cut one large-headed Chrysanthemum and insert it temporarily into the frame, as before; then attach the bump to the frame with 6mm pot tape, using extra hairpins if necessary. Do not make the foam bump the same width as the letter, as this will distort the lettering when the basing is added later. Pin the two layers of ribbon along the edges of the foam using decorative pins to secure. Screw in the clips, using the drawn guide line on the back of the foam. Soak the letter and clip it onto the frame; check the spacing and adjust as required. Traditional box pleating or a foliage edge can be used as an alternative.

2. Cut and grade the Chrysanthemums as before. Starting at the tips of the foam, insert three small heads at a 45-degree angle so they do not extend over the width – this will help keep the corners crisp. Take care when basing around any 'holes' in the letters, as it is very easy to fill these in so that it is hard to distinguish the letter; it may be necessary to use smaller heads for this.

3. Insert a row of medium-headed Chrysanthemums all round the outer edge – bond them closely to each other but without overlapping; the centre 'eyes' of these Chrysanthemums should 'look' into your face. Continue this process until the first row is completed.

Frame examples.

Frame examples.

Clip lettering attachment.

Screw-in lettering attachment.

1. Add the bump and attach the ribbon.

2. Add small-headed Chrysanthemums to the inside edges of the letter.

the bump in a staggered line. Note that the flowers in the spray on a based letter must be small so that the spray does not interfere with the legibility of the letter. Not every letter needs a spray of flowers – look at the length of the word created, and decide which of the letters requires this.

7. Finally mist spray the finished design and insert the tribute card.

ALTERNATIVE DESIGN IDEAS
The foam could be based in a different material, for example Molucella, Hydrangea, Gypsophila. Alternatively it could be based with white chrysanthemums and a different colour chrysanthemum on the top, which would help the legibility of the letter. Different colours of polyribbon and different ribbon edging could be used, such as box pleating or foliage edging, or different flowers, or colours of flower in the spray – for example mini Orchids, Eustoma, spray Chrysanthemums.

3. The first row of Chrysanthemums.

4. The top layer of Chrysanthemums.

5. The foliage is inserted as the base of the spray.

6. The flowers are added to the spray.

7. Alternative colours could be used in the design.

4. Add the top row: the 'eyes' of these Chrysanthemums 'face upwards to the sky'. Bond them closely together.

5. Add the foliage to the bump in the proportions two thirds Ruscus lengthways, and one third either side of Arachniodes adiantiformis (leather leaf);

add these foliages until the foam bump is nearly concealed and the profile is raised at the centre. Add the filler flower Solidaster throughout.

6. Support wire the Rosa using the external wire method (see Wiring Techniques at the beginning of Chapter 6 for guidance), then insert them into

Loose Open-Style Letters

Making letters using mixed flowers and foliages can make them harder to distinguish, so take great care in the way colours and textures are used, so as to enhance legibility.

MATERIALS
Fresh flowers and foliages
Five Rosa 'Sphinx' (focal flower)
Five Germini (focal flower)
One stem Ruscus racemosa
Two Arachniodes adiantiformis
One Solidaster (filler flower)
One Limonium (filler flower)
Three Rosmarinus
One Asparagus umbellatus

Sundries
Plastic-backed letter 'P'
Florist's knife and scissors

SUITABILITY
As before.

Storage

As before.

METHOD
1. Soak the frame. Cut a selection of foliages and insert these round the edge of the letter P: this helps to define the outline, but take care as you dress the inside edge of the P not to fill in the hole.

2. Insert the foliages into the remainder of the frame, putting different textures next to each other to maximize their impact.

3. Support wire the focal flowers using external wiring (see Wiring Techniques at the beginning of Chapter 6). Cut the Germinis all the same length so that they stand slightly proud of the foliages and insert them, then cut the Rosas all the same length and insert them, but so

they are slightly recessed against the Germinis.

4. Add the filler flowers, Solidaster and Limonium, in equal measure so as to obtain visual balance.

5. Check that all the foam is covered, and that all the materials are secure and none is damaged. A nice option is to add modelino cane as a decorative feature. Attach to the frame. Insert the tribute card.

ALTERNATIVE DESIGN IDEAS
You could create a ribbon edge. Other focal flowers could be Dianthus, or Chrysanthemum blooms.

1. Mixed foliage edging.

2. The completed foliage frame.

3. The focal flowers are added.

4. The secondary flowers are added.

5. Attach the letter to the frame.

Alternative Basing Designs

MATERIALS

Fresh flowers and foliages

Five Gloriosa rothschildiana (focal flower)
Eight Moluccella (basing flower)
One Ruscus racemosa
Three Leucadendron
Four Liriope muscari (Lily grass)
Medium Hedera helix (ivy) leaves (edging material)
Hedera helix (ivy) trails

Sundries

24cm (9.5in) bio-wreath ring frame
Small piece of wet foam (for the bump)
String
Florist's knife and scissors
Secateurs

SUITABILITY

A contemporary formal funeral design suitable for a young or trendy individual of either gender – with a different colour of focal flower, the design could be more gender specific. This is a formal design normally sent to close family or friends. The choice of a bio-degradable frame and the use of bio-degradable materials make this design suitable for an individual who was environmentally aware. (Note that although wet foam is not completely bio-degradable, it does allow plant material to grow through it.)

Storage

Store at room temperature because of the Gloriosa.

METHOD

1. Cut a small piece of wet foam and tie it to the bio frame with string; at a later stage the spray will be fashioned on this. Make sure this foam piece is not wider than the width of the frame, and that it is high enough once the top layer of basing is inserted. Cut the medium Hedera helix leaves, choosing leaves that are big enough to be seen once the basing is in place, and insert them round the inner and outer edge of the frame; they may need stitching.

2. Cut up Moluccella as shown in the photograph, cutting just above each flower floret; this will be the basing material.

1. Preparing the frame with Hedera leaf edging.

2. Cutting up the Moluccella.

3. The first row of Moluccella.

4. The inner row of Moluccella.

5. The top row of Moluccella.

6. Inserting the foliage to make the spray.

3. Insert the prepared Moluccella round the outer circle of the wreath frame. Bond the materials close together leaving no gaps and so the foam does not show.

4. Continue until you have gone all round the outer edge, then repeat the process for the inner edge (making sure not to conceal the hole in the middle of the wreath).

5. Complete the basing process by adding a final row of Moluccella along the top of the wreath ring.

6. Create the main spray by cutting Ruscus, Leucadendron and Hedera helix, and adding this foliage to the prepared foam bump (see the project Based-Style Wreath Ring at the beginning of the previous section above for guidance on proportions). Link the card spray to the main spray with two stems of Liriope muscari (lily grass); add a couple of grass loops into the main spray.

7. Add the Gloriosa (focal flower), one at each end of the main spray and two back-to-back in the middle to create a focal area of interest. Opposite the spray insert a Gloriosa and a Leucadendron: this is the card spray where the tribute card is inserted.

8. Check that all the foam is concealed, that there are no damaged materials, and that they are all secure. Insert the tribute card. Mist the finished design.

ALTERNATIVE DESIGN IDEAS
For the foliage edging you could use Galax leaves, Camilla leaves, Pittosporum, Asparagus umbellatus (ming fern).
As an alternative choice of flower for the basing you could have Hydrangea, Eryngium heads, Gypsophila, flat moss (Plagiothecium undulatum) bunn moss (Leucobryum glaucum).
For focal flowers you could try Rosa, Cybidium orchid, Dendrobium orchid, small Allium, Chincherinchee (Ornithogalum).

8. The finished design.

7. With the flowers added.

Chapter 9
Seasonal Designs

One of the joys of being a florist is the change of products throughout the seasons: in spring the bulb flowers, Narcissus and Hyacinthus; in summer the many meadow flowers such as Centaurea (cornflowers), Nigella and Delphinium; in autumn the rich colours of Kniphofia (red hot poker) and Dahlia; and finally winter, with the textures of blue pine and brightly hued flowers such as the Hippeastrum and the glittering array of materials to support Christmas time. Due to modern growing and cultivating techniques, most flowers are available, at a cost, throughout the whole year. However, working with flowers and foliages when they are naturally available is not only working with fresh materials at their best, their natural growing season, but also when they are at their most reasonable price.

Easter Gift Box

MATERIALS
Fresh flowers and foliages
Four Ruscus
One Eucalyptus parvifolia
Seven Freesia 'Rapid Yellow'
Ten Tulipa of mixed colours

Sundries
One gift box
One cellophane
One block of wet foam

SUITABILITY
This gift box of flowers is suitable for a variety of uses, according to the accessories it carries: eggs at Easter time, but it can also be presented as a spring gift box, a cheer-up gift, a mother's day present, or for a birthday.

Storage (florist)
Store this design in a cool area, and in the dark because Tulipa are phototropic and will move to the light, until delivery or collection. Top up the foam with water as required, and mist according to the materials used.

Care (customer)
Avoid placing this gift box in direct sunlight, in draughts, near fruit, or where they would be affected by fluctuating temperatures. Top up the foam every few days with tepid water.

METHOD
1. Line the gift box with cellophane and cut the foam to fit; then soak the foam.

2. Cut the Ruscus and Eucalyptus into short lengths and insert into the foam, making sure the lower placements are angled so they conceal the join where the foam meets the lip of the box. Create a pleasing profile.

3. Cut and add the Tulipa and Freesia: they should be higher than the foliage in profile, and placed so as to create a visual balance. Remember that even

after cutting Tulipa continues to grow, so cut these a little shorter.

4. Add the eggs, distributing them evenly throughout the design. If the box has a lid, place it at an angle and secure with 90mm-gauge pins; if it has a cord, pull this tight.

5. Check that all the materials are secure, and that none is damaged, and that the foam is concealed. Mist carefully so as not to spoil the paper gift box.

1. Line the box and add the foam.

LEFT: Halloween design.

2. Insert the foliages.

3. Add the flowers.

4. Add the Easter accessories.

ALTERNATIVE DESIGN IDEAS
Gift boxes come in a variety of colours, and by adding the appropriate accessories, many different designs can be created for all sorts of different occasions – for example, Valentine's Day and Christmas designs can be made by adding heart picks or Christmas baubles, and adding different accessories gives a variety of possibilities to the creative opportunities.

Christmas gift box.

Halloween Design

MATERIALS
Fresh flowers and foliages
One carved pumpkin
Two Physalis
One Salix (twisted willow)
Two Cotinus
Four Rosmarinus officinalis (rosemary)
Four chilli peppers
Three Gerberas 'Classic Fabio Orange'
Five Pennisetum

Sundries
One tray
One third of a block of wet foam
Decorative headed pins
Black aluminium wire
Pot tape
Florist's knife and scissors

Suitability

This design would be suitable for any Halloween décor: a party, a restaurant or hotel reception table, as an 'in store' feature, or for a window display.

Storage (florist)

Store in a dark, cool area until delivery or collection, top up the foam with water as required, and mist if appropriate to the materials used.

Care (customer)

Avoid placing this design in direct sunlight, in draughts, near fruit, or where it would be affected by fluctuating temperatures. Top up the foam every few days with tepid water.

METHOD

1. Carve the facial expression, and carve out the inside of the pumpkin (to avoid premature rotting). Cut out a hole in the top of the pumpkin big enough for a foam tray to fit snugly. It is very important that the hole is a snug fit – if it is slightly too big, when the design is complete the tray together with the weight of the wet foam and fresh materials could fall into the middle of the pumpkin. Place the pumpkin on a decorative plate.

2. Pot tape the foam into the tray, and fit the tray into the top of the pumpkin.

3. One option to this design is to include a hat – pin the hat into the foam using decorative headed pins, allowing for most of the foam to show so that fresh materials can be added.

4. Place the Salix (twisted willow) into the foam – this is to add height to the arrangement, though be careful not to conceal the 'face' of the pumpkin.

5. Support wire Physalis heads using the single leg mount method (see Wiring Techniques at the beginning of Chapter 6). Wire the support-wired Physalis heads to the willow to create a line of colour.

6. Add cut rosemary stems into the foam to simulate hair, grouping it at each side of the foam.

7. Add Cotinus to the foam to give a good coverage and to raise the profile.

8. Insert the Gerberas (the focal flowers) just off centre to achieve an interesting visual balance.

9. Insert the chilli peppers (the filler material) on either side of the Gerbera to create a diagonal line and increase the visual impact. One option is to construct a 'broom' – bunch together several stems of Pennisetum tied with black aluminium wire, and place these at the base of the pumpkin head. Insert a battery-operated light into the pumpkin so that it shines through the 'eyes'. Place the design on a decorative plate.

1. Carve out the pumpkin.

2. Attach the container and the foam to the pumpkin.

3. Add the hat.

4. Insert the Salix.

7. Insert the rest of the foliages.

8. Insert the flowers.

5. Wire on the Physalis heads.

6. Insert the foliages for 'hair'.

9. The finished design with the 'broom'.

ALTERNATIVE IDEAS

A pumpkin, melon or water melon could be substituted as a container for a tropical party design. Instead of Gerberas, large-headed orange Rosa could be used as focal flowers, or Helianthus (sunflower) – although these are very thirsty and the design would need to be frequently topped up with water.

....

Christmas Door Wreath

MATERIALS
Fresh flowers and foliages
Sphagnum moss
Three stems of blue pine
Sprigs of Ilex (holly)
Sprigs of tree Hedera (ivy)
One red Cornus
1.5m red ribbon
Four pine cones
Three felt snowflake decoration
Ten small Christmas baubles

Sundries
Wreath wrap
Mossing pins
56mm reel wire
10in copper wreath ring
90mm wires
120mm wire
Floral tape

Suitability

To be hung on the door during the celebration of Christmas. Alternatively it could be used as a Christmas or funeral tribute if the decoration choice was appropriate.

Storage (florist)

Store the wreath in a dark, cool area until delivery or collection.

Care (customer)

Hang the door wreath in the desired position.

METHOD

An alternative medium can be created out of sphagnum moss. Bind moss on to a copper frame: the moist moss acts in a similar way to foam by helping foliages stay fresh. (Before the introduction of floral foam all designs that needed medium were constructed in this way.)

1. Create 'sausages' of moss by rolling a bundle of sphagnum moss together. Then bind the moss to the copper frame using 56-gauge reel wire; bind it on tightly and ensure there are no gaps between 'sausages'. Once this task has been completed, trim over the moss with scissors until the surface is smooth. It is essential that the wire is bound tightly so that when 'trimming' the moss you do not cut through the wire.

2. Cut and sort blue pine into suitable lengths, identified as 'fingers', 'small hands' and 'large hands'; defoliate the ends so they can be bound as tightly as possible to the moss ring.

3. Cast on the 56-gauge reel wire by poking one end into the moss ring and tightly binding it round a few times. Start to bind on the blue pine: lay the 'fingers' tight against the inside of the moss ring, and at the same time the 'small hands' on the outside of the ring; bind as tightly as possible over the defoliated stem.

4. Position the pieces for the next layer of pine on top of the previous bound pine so they conceal the binding-on process.

5. Lay the large 'hands' on the front of the moss ring and bind as before.

6. Continue this process until all the moss ring is covered neatly with blue pine with no gaps, making sure that all the pine is secure, and that you have not 'lost' either the outer or the inner

circular outline shape.

7. Tape 120mm-gauge wire to make the hook by which to hang the finished wreath (if it is intended as a tribute a hook will not be needed). Turn the wreath over and push the covered wire through the moss, making sure that the wire feeds under the copper frame; then repeat this with the other end of the wire until you are left with a loop and

1. The mossed frame.

2. Grading the blue pine.

3. Binding on the pine.

4. Binding on the next layer of pine.

6. The finished foliage wreath.

9. ...and continuing all the way round.

5. Binding on the front layer of pine.

7. Making the hook to hang the wreath.

10. The finished backing.

8. Starting to wreath wrap the back of the ring...

11. Support wire the Christmas decorations.

12. Wire in the decorations.

13. The finished design.

two end wires. Complete the hook by wrapping the ends of the wires up and round the hook; cut off the excess wire and then tape for neatness and to conceal any sharp wires.

8. Start to wreath wrap the back of the ring using mossing pins to secure the wrap – pin these horizontally into the frame, starting on the inside.

9. Continue round the ring using a zig zag folding action: secure the wrap with two pins, then fold it over and secure with the next two pins, fold it over again, and so on round the ring.

10. Continue this process until all the back is covered. This has a two-fold purpose: it will protect the door from damage, and it will help to keep the moisture in the moss and the foliages hydrated on the moss ring.

11. Using the double leg mount method (see Wiring Techniques at the beginning of Chapter 6) with a heavy wire 90mm, support wire the decoration pieces: these could be additional foliages, for example Ilex (holly) or tree

Hedera, and attach Christmas decorations such as ribbon, baubles, cinnamon sticks and pine cones.

12. Turn the wreath ring the right side up. It is helpful to tie a piece of ribbon on to the hook so that you know which way up the wreath will be when it is hanging (you could find that you decorate the wreath only to find that the top of your design was not in the right place once it was hanging). Insert the decorations into the top of wreath through the pine into the moss, then bend them back on themselves for extra security. Carry on decorating until you have achieved the effect you want.

13. Check that all the wired-on decoration is secure, and that no wires have

protruded through the wreath wrap – if this has happened, use pliers and bend the offending wires back into the moss frame.

ALTERNATIVE IDEAS
This same moss process can be applied to create a floristry medium on other copper shapes, for example crosses, letters, three-dimensional animal frames, even tailor-made copper frames. The copper frames and binding wire will eventually rust, so creating this style of floristry medium is more environmentally friendly, or they can be reused.

Foliage alternatives could be Hedera helix, Cupressus, holly, myrtle, Buxus sempervirens, laurel.

Traditional Christmas Advent Design

MATERIALS

Fresh flowers and foliages
Two stems of blue pine
Four spray Rosa 'Avalanche' (focal flower)
Three Eryngium
One Pinus
One Ilex 'Blue Prince'
Assorted pine cones
One white glittered birch

Sundries
12in wreath ring
Four candles
Four candle holders
2m Christmas wired ribbon
Flower glitter, flower glue

SUITABILITY

This design is a Christmas table arrangement that celebrates advent, each candle to be lit on each of the four Sundays prior to Christmas day. It can be placed on a high or a low table, but is more suitable for round tables. It can be used for functions, for a Christmas wedding or as a table decoration for a low table in a hotel reception (but check with the venue whether candles are allowed).

Storage (florist)
Store this design in a dark, cool area until delivery or collection. Top up the foam as required, and mist according to the materials used. Ensure that the candle care card is included with the design.

1. Push the candles firmly into the candle holders.

2. Start inserting the outer foliage edging

3. Add the top layer of foliage.

4. The finished foliaged wreath.

5. Fill any gaps with additional foliages – here, Ilex and Pinus.

6. Add the flowers and the ribbon decororation.

Care (customer)

Avoid placing the design in direct sunlight, in draughts, near fruit, or where it may be affected by fluctuating temperatures. Top up the foam once a week with tepid water.

METHOD

1. Soak the foam. Put the candles into candle holders, and insert these firmly into the foam, spaced evenly round the wreath ring. Ensure that the candles are secure and upright.

2. Cut up and sort the blue pine as before, into 'fingers, and 'small' and 'large hands'; defoliate the end of the stems (see Door Wreath, above, for guidance) to allow firm insertion into the foam ring. Start by inserting the foliages on the outer edge of the ring, using the same sized 'fingers' and pushing them into the foam at a slight downward angle (on to the table) and clockwise; continue until the outer ring is covered. Repeat this process on the inner ring, being careful not to 'fill in' the hole of the wreath – use shorter pieces on the inside edge.

3. Next, insert the 'hand-sized' pieces of the pine into and around the top of the wreath ring, placing them at an acute angle, with each hand on top of the previous one to obscure the insertion point.

4. Continue in this way until you have covered the foam.

5. Now fill any remaining foam spaces with the other foliages, Ilex and Pinus, cut to appropriate lengths and inserted into any gaps between the pine.

6. Add the focal flowers – in this design Rosa – at regular intervals round the wreath ring. (The cut length of the Rosa should stand proud of the foliage base.)

7. The finished design.

Make the ribbon bows and pin these into the foam, making certain that nothing flammable is too close to the candles.

7. Cut the flower heads of the Eryngium long enough to be inserted into the foam but so they are still visible through the pine. Add the glitter twigs. A nice option is to spray flower glue on to the rose heads and apply glitter.

8. Check that all the foam is covered, that all the flower, foliage and decoration items are secure, and that the flammable items are not too close to the candles. Attach a candle care card to the design.

ALTERNATIVE IDEAS

For a cheaper Christmas alternative, rather than using fresh flowers, which can be very expensive at this time of year, use Christmas baubles or other Christmas decorations. For a non-Christmas design, replace the blue pine with mixed foliages: Hedera helix, Arachniodes adiantiformis (leather leaf), and/or Eucalyptus. You could change the colour of the candles for a themed anniversary candle arrangement, for example silver for a silver wedding anniversary, red for a ruby wedding anniversary, and so on.

Contemporary Christmas Advent Design

MATERIALS
Fresh flowers and foliages
1$\frac{1}{2}$ stems of blue pine
Four cones

Sundries
12in wreath ring
Hot glue/glue gun
Decorative headed pins
Four red advent candles
2m decorative floral organza (floral organza is colourfast)
1.5m flat aluminium wire
Ten decorative Christmas baubles

SUITABILITY
As the previous project, Traditional Christmas Advent Design.

Storage and care
As the previous project, Traditional Christmas Advent Design.

METHOD
1. Remove the staples from the underside of a polyfoam-based wreath ring – cut down the seam on one side and then cut the opposite side. Cut carefully, because the straighter the cut, the easier it will be to glue together. Position the two halves of the ring into an 'S' shape.

2. Hot glue the two halves together and replace the staples.

3. For extra security and before the glue has set, insert some wooden skewers diagonally across the newly glued seam. Cut the skewers so they are flush with the foam, and then pot tape completely round the seam, both on top and underneath.

4. Pin the organza using decorative headed pins into the sides of the 'S' shape, gathering it to make pin tucks to form a pleasing gathered edge. Soak the

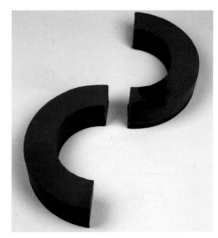

1. Cut the wreath ring in half.

2. Glue the new seam together with hot glue.

3. Reinforce the new seam with wooden picks.

4. Pin on the organza.

5. Prepare the candles.

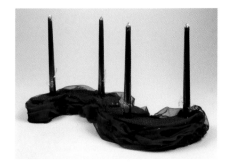

6. Insert the candles.

7. Add the foliage.

8. The finished foliage.

foam. An alternative look can be achieved by replacing the organza with strips of aspidistra leaves.

5. Prepare the candles to insert into foam – cut wooden skewers so they are a little longer that the depth of the foam, and secure them to the base of the candle with 12mm pot tape (or you can use candle holders).

6. Insert the candles into the desired positions: make sure that maximum security is achieved by using wooden skewers – you will be able to hear these 'crunch' into the polyfoam base.

7. Cut and defoliate blue pine, sorting them into medium 'hands' and 'fingers' (see the previous project for guidance). Insert them at an acute angle into the foam.

8. Place blue pine at each end, working your way to the middle until all the foam is covered.

9. Make some organza roses and add them to the design with the leg mount method. Make some decorative metal swirls with flat aluminium, and insert them into the foam. Add wired red

cornus bundles and wired cones. Finish off the design with wired Christmas baubles.

10. Check that all the foam is covered, that all the flower, foliage and decoration items are secure, and that no flammable item is too close to any of the candles. Attach a candle care card to the design.

ALTERNATIVE IDEAS
See the previous project, Traditional Christmas Advent Design.

9. Add the Christmas decorations.

Christmas Candle Design

MATERIALS
Fresh flowers and foliages
Two stems of blue pine
Four aspidistra leaves
Six cones

Sundries
8in posy pad
Glass hurricane lamp
115/50 candle, and a blob of florist's fix to secure it
Assorted wires
Glitter spray
Glitter
1m ribbon
Christmas baubles: six silver, four green, eight slender silver drops
Diamante pins

SUITABILITY
This Christmas arrangement can be placed on a low coffee table, a long dining table, or on a sideboard or dresser. It may be used at a Christmas wedding, or at Christmas corporate parties.

Storage (florist)
Store the design in a dark, cool area until delivery or collection. Top up the foam with water as required, and mist according to the materials used.

Care (customer)
Avoid placing the design in direct sunlight, in draughts, near fruit, or where it would be affected by fluctuating temperatures. Top up the foam once a week with tepid water.

METHOD
1. Soak the posy pad. Using two paper-covered wires, wind the wires round the neck of the hurricane lamp, and twist tightly together; repeat on the opposite side. Cut the wire so that it is no longer that the depth of the posy pad. Attach the lamp to the posy pad, pushing the wires into the pad and firmly into the base of the polyfoam base. Check that they have not gone all the way through the pad.

2. Cut and sort the blue pine into appropriate lengths (see the earlier door wreath project for guidance), and insert these into the foam at the opposite ends of the posy pad; angle the first placements on to the table.

3. Then keep layering the pine until you have covered both sides.

4. Next insert the stems of two of the aspidistra leaves into the pad, then fold, gather and secure with decorative pins until you have covered all the foam. Repeat this procedure on the opposite side.

5. Using the leg mount method, prepare the required Christmas decorations and insert them securely into the posy pad; add the decorative ribbon bows. Put a couple of blobs of florist's fix on the bottom of the candle to prevent it falling over, and put it into the hurricane lamp.

6. Check that all the foam is covered, and that the foliage and decorations are secure. Attach a candle care card to the design.

ALTERNATIVE IDEAS
Instead of just Christmas decorations, use fresh flowers, too. For a non-Christmas design, replace the blue pine with mixed foliages, Hedera helix, Arachniodes adiantiformis (leather leaf), and/or Eucalyptus and assorted flowers. Change the colour of the lamp and add sand in the base to secure the candle for a 'high

1. Wiring up the hurricane lamp.

3. The outer sections of blue pine completed.

2. Insert the outer foliages.

4. Pin and fold the aspidistra leaves.

5. Add the Christmas decorations.

summer' look; to complete the beach look,
add some shells. (See Chapter 7 Function
Designs for a summer flower
interpretation.)

Christmas Garland

MATERIALS
Fresh flowers and foliages
Two stems of blue pine
One stem of Pinus
Three cones

Sundries
Strong garden string
Fourteen gold baubles
Five Christmas stars
3m ribbon

SUITABILITY
This design can be hung over a fireplace, on a stair banister or on a column, placed on a buffet table for Christmas decoration, or to adorn a Christmas wedding.

Storage (florist)
Store the design in a dark, cool area until delivery or collection. Mist according to the materials used.

Care (customer)
Avoid placing the design in direct sunlight, in draughts, near fruit, or where it would be affected by fluctuating temperatures. Mist it every couple of days (take care of interior walls when misting).

METHOD
1. Measure the finished placement – for example the fireplace – to determine the length of the garland (see the garland project in Chapter 7, Function Designs for guidance). Cut the string a little longer than required to allow for attachment when it is finished. If you are making a full and long garland, double the string for extra strength, or

1. Bind on the foliages.

2. Wire in the cones.

3. Wire in the Christmas decorations.

4. The finished design.

use a piping cord. (The materials for this project made a 1.5m length of garland.) When constructing a garland, tie each end of string to a firm fixture to keep it taut so the materials can be bound on firmly. Cut the foliage into similar lengths, defoliating the bottom of each stem. Wrap the 52mm-gauge reel wire round the string, then bind on the foliage, starting at one end and securing each one; try to make an all-round shape by binding all round the string, so that each new foliage sprig overlaps the binding point of the previous sprig. Repeat this construction method until the desired length has been achieved.

2. Next add the decoration. Support wire the cones, and wire them onto the garland at regular intervals.

3. Add the wired baubles.

4. Continue to add the decorations, wiring them on to the garland, creating a regular pattern.

5. Check that all the wired decorations are secure, and the wires are neatly finished to avoid scratching the furniture. Mist the foliage.

ALTERNATIVE IDEAS
Try combining the Christmas decorations with fresh flowers: place individual flowers into plastic phials, and wiring the phials onto the garland. This is best done when the garland is in its finished position so that you know where best to place the flowers (see the garland project in Chapter 7, Function Designs). For a non-Christmas design replace the blue pine with mixed foliages: Hedera helix, gaultheria shallon and/ or Eucalyptus.

Glossary

Achromatic colours: black, grey and white are regarded as neutral colours within floral design.

Backing: the method used to cover the back of a mossed design, either a tribute or wreath, to keep in the moisture and prevent damage to the coffin or door.

Balance, actual and visual: a design constructed so that it does not fall over (actual balance) and that colours, textures and forms are equally placed throughout the design (visual balance).

Basing: term applied to covering a medium in one material, the material is bonded closely together e.g. Chrysanthemums for a tribute but still retaining the required outline shape.

Binding point: describes the one point where materials are bound together. This can apply to wired designs, e.g. corsages, or fresh designs where the stems are tied together.

Botrytis: bacteria that can form on fresh material, causing decay and shortening the life span of flowers.

Bump: term applied to a piece of foam or mechanic that is used to create a spray of fresh flowers on a funeral tribute

Conditioning: procedure in which fresh materials are prepared for sale.

Distinction: this is achieved by unusual use of plant material, e.g. plaiting of leaves.

Ethylene gas: the colourless gas given off by decaying flower materials and fruit. It causes irreparable damage to flowers.

External wiring: wiring technique describing a wire that is inserted into the base of the flower head and wound around the stem.

Facing: method of manoeuvring leaf or flower material to conceal binding points or mechanics.

Filler flower: term applied to a flower with many tiny heads, generally used to support a dominant floral placement.

Focal area: the main area or areas of interest within a floristry design.

Focal flower: flower or flowers that have the most dominance within a design.

Greening up: term applied to creating coverage of foliage onto a base.

Mechanics: describes materials such as foam, wire, mossing pins, etc.

Mount wiring: technique of strengthening a stem by adding a wire to it, thus creating a false stem that can be then inserted into a medium or a binding point.

Pipping: a wiring technique whereby individual flowers are wired by threading the wire up through stem and flower head, bending the wire over and pulling it deep back into the flower head.

Recession: describes lower placements within designs or the use of receding colours to add visual dimensions to any design.

Secondary flowers: flowers that play a supporting role within designs; generally this flower is not as expensive as a focal flower.

Semi-internal wiring: the technique of inserting a wire into the stem 5cm (2in) below the head and then winding it around the stem.

Stay wire: technique of wiring individual flowers and foliages onto a prepared wire to strengthen and support them.

Stitching: wiring technique that supports individual leaves to allow for more flexibility within floral designs.

Support wiring: technique of strengthening the stem by adding a wire to it.

Unit: fresh materials that are bound together. There are three different types of unit – branching, ribbed and natural.

Wiring: the use of wire for control, support and anchorage of plant materials.

Index

A

achromatic colour 25
Advent design 182–186
    modern 184–186
    traditional 182–184
Alice band headdress 104–111
    using floral glue 109–111
    wired construction 104–106
arrangements 59–79
    asymmetrical arrangement 67–70
    basket arrangement 73–74
    candle arrangement 71–72
    coloured foam arrangement 76–78
    container without a handle – posy style 74–75
    differences between modern and traditional designs 77
    line arrangement 62–64
    modern arrangement 64
    packaging and transport 60–61
    parallel arrangement 79
    symmetrical arrangement 65–67
analogous colour 26
aqua-pack hostess bouquet 43–45
asymmetrical arrangement 67–70

B

bacteria 17
balance principle 31–32
based styles 158–170
botrytis 17
branching unit 84
bridal designs
    single flower – tied construction 86–88
    natural posy – tied construction 88–89
    bridal holders – advantages and disadvantages 90
    bridal holder – mixed flowers 90–92
    bridal holder – with fancy frame 92–94
    bridal posy – wired construction 101–102
bridesmaid novelties 113–117
buffet designs 131–135
    candle arrangement 71–72
    candelabra arrangement 133–134
    hurricane lamp arrangement 134–135
    vase arrangement 131–132
buttonhole 93–96
    standard 93–95
    non standard 95–96

C

cake top arrangements 126–129
    in foam 128–129
candle arrangements 133–135, 182–187
    candelabra 133–134
    hurricane lamp design 134–135
    Advent design contemporary 184–186
    Advent design traditional 182–184
    Christmas candle arrangement 186–187
Christmas designs 179–189
    Christmas door wreath 179–181
    Christmas advent traditional 182–184
    Christmas advent contemporary 184–186
    Christmas candle design 186–187
    Christmas garland 188–189
Christmas gift box 177
church flowers 120–130
    garlands 124–127
    pew ends 120–124
    topiary flowers 129–130
chrysanthemums – based 159
circlet headdress 103–104
colour – element 23–28
    association 24
    modifying 25
colour harmonies 25–28
    analogous 26
    complementary 26
    contrast 27
    monochromatic 25
    near complementary 27
    polychromatic 26
    split complementary 27
    tetradic 28
    triadic 28
colour wheel 24
cone wrap 35–40
conditioning flowers 17
    botrytis 17
    environmental conditions 17–18
    ethylene gas 17
    hollow stems 19
    latex stems 19
    prioritize conditioning 19
    revival methods 21
    semi woody stems 19
    woody stems 19
containers 13, 59–61
    advantages and disadvantages 61
contrasting colour harmony 27
contrast principle 32
complementary colour harmony 26
corsages 96–112
    line corsage 96–99
    posy corsage 99–101

    glued corsage 108–109
    wrist corsage 111–112
cross shaped tributes 151–153, 165–167
    loose open design 151–153
    based design 165–167
cushion tribute based 167–168
cutting tools 11

D

dominance principle 31
double-ended spray for funeral tributes 139–141
double leg mount 84

E

Easter gift box 175–176
edging for tributes 138
elements of design 23
    colour 23–28
    form 28
    texture 23
    space 29
    line 30
ethylene gas 17

F

fixing tools 12
flat bouquet, wrapped 40–42
floristry wires 12
    decorative wires 13
    reel wire 12
    stub wires 12
    wires and their uses 82
flower food 18
foam 59
    coloured foam
    dry foam
    how to use foam
    wet foam
foliage bag 113–115
form element 29
function designs 119–135
    cake decorations 126–129
        design requirements 126–128
        cake design in foam 128–129
    garlanding – measuring up 124
        foam frame construction 125–126
        foliage construction 126–127
    pew ends advantages and disadvantages 120
        tied 123–124
        foam 121–123
    site visit 119
    tools for off site use 119

    topiary 129–131
funeral flower etiquette 139
funeral flowers and tributes
    basing 158–170, 172–173
    edging 138
    order requirements 137
    mediums 137

G

garlands 125–127, 188–189
    foam 125–126
    wired 126–127, 188–189
gift wrapping 35
glue 106
    hot guns 106
    floristry glue 106
glued designs
    corsage – glued construction 108–109
    hair band – glued construction 109–111
    wristlet – glued construction 111–112

H

hair comb – wired construction 106–108
Hallowe'en design 177–179
handbag
    foliage construction 113–117
    sisal construction 115–116
hand tied designs 35–54, 86–89
harmony principle 31
headwear requirements – design choice, flower choice, order requirements 102
    Alice band glued 109–111
    Alice band wired 104–106
    circlet wired 103–104
    hair comb wired 106–108
health and safety 14
heart shaped tributes
    loose open design 149–151
    based design 163–165
hollow stems conditioning 19
hurricane lamp design
    summer wedding design 134–135
    Christmas design 186–187

I

insurance 15
    employer's liability insurance 15
    public liability insurance 15

L

leaf manipulation 55–57
    broad leaf 56
    palm plaiting 55–56
    threading 57

leg mounts wiring 84
    single leg mount 84
    double leg mount 84
letter shaped tributes 168–171
    loose open design 169–171
    based design 169–170
line element 30
luminosity 25

M

monochromatic colour harmony 25
Moluccella basing 172–173

N

natural posy 88–89
natural unit 84
near complementary colour harmony 27
neutral colours 25

O

ordering flowers and foliage 10–11

P

packaging 35, 60
parallel 78–79
peak periods 8–9
pew ends
    tied construction 123–124
    foam construction 121–123
pillow shaped tributes 167–168
pinning 138
pipping 82–83
plant and flower nomenclature 10
polychromatic colour harmony 26
pomander 116–117
posy pad shaped tributes
    loose open design 147–149
    based design 161–162
principles of design 30–33
    balance 31
    contrast 32
    dominance 30
    harmony 31
    proportion 31
    rhythm 33
    scale 32
proportion principle 31

R

revival methods 21
rhythm principle 33
ribbed unit wiring 85
    wired circlet 103
    wired Alice band 105
ribbon edging in tributes 138, 150, 151, 160, 167
rubbish disposal 21

S

seasonal designs 175–189
scale principle 32
single ended spray 142–143
single ended spray with stems 144–147
single flower wrapping 35
single leg mount 84
sisal bag 115–116
space element 29
sphagnum moss 179
spiral method 43, 47, 49, 53
split complementary colour harmony 27
stay wire 103, 105
stock rotation 21
support wiring 82
symmetrical arrangement 65–67
sympathy basket 153–155

T

table arrangements
    buffet table 131
tetradic colour harmony 28
texture in design element 23
textured pillow 155–156
tied designs 35–54
    tied sheaf 156–158
    single flower – cellophane wrapped 35–36
    cone wrap – craft wrapped 37–38
    cone wrap – cello wrapped 38–40
    flat pack 40–42
    tied bouquet – mixed flower aqua packed 43–45
    tied bouquet – grouped textured 45–47
    tied bridal bouquet – single flower 86–88
    tied bridal bouquet – natural posy 88–89
    tied bouquet – self made frames 48–51
    tied bouquet – bought frame 51–52
    tied bouquet – limited handtied 52–55
tools of the trade 10
topiary 129–131
triadic colour harmony 28
tribute cards 137
tying aids 12

U

units
    natural 84
    ribbed 84
    branch 84

V

vase arrangement 131–133

W

wedding designs 81–117, 120–125
wedding order 81
wholesale and retail prices 10
wired bridal work
    advantages and disadvantages 85
    Alice band 104–106
    bridal posy wired construction 101–102
    circlet 103–104
    corsage – line style 96–99
        posy style 99–101
    hair comb 106–108
    non-standard buttonhole 95–96
    standard buttonhole 94–95
    wrist corsage 106–108
wires – and their uses 82
wiring techniques 82–84
    support wiring 82
    cross stitching 83
    external wiring 83
    internal wiring 82
    pipping 82
    semi-internal wiring 83
    stitching 83
    mount wiring 84
        single leg mount 84
        double leg mount 84
    units
        branching unit 84
        natural unit 84
        ribbed unit 84
woody stems 19
wrist corsages 111–112
    corsage wired construction 112–113
    corsage glued construction 111–112
wreath – Christmas door wreath 179–181
wreath shaped tributes
    loose open design 146–147
    based design – Chrysanthemum 159–161
    based design – Moluccella 172–173